CONTENTS

The test	2
Beaver country	7
Uncle Sam's travel	11
The real navy	15
A slip in the deep	22
That sucking sound	27
Navy watch business	31
Wild blue yonder	37
The Marine affair	44
Crusty Shellback	48
Tin can sailors	52
The contract	55
Miracle at Kansas University	62
Dealing with doctors	66
Ready for sea	70
Mother of all journeys	75
Gardiners Bay (AVP-39)	84
Nationalist Navy	89
Station Ship Hong Kong	96
The paper tiger	101
Spuds and slit skirts	108

Mary Soo	114
Hamilton County (LST-802)	118
Load list from hell	123
Wooden ships: iron men	131
The wardroom rat	136
Honolulu hang-up	140
Contrast in cultures	144
Typhoon T	152
Cumshaw navy	158
Sayonara US Navy	168

THE TEST

When I was a kid, I was asked a hundred times "What do you want to do when you grow up?" Mostly I remember the questions, as I had no good answers. My folks were both school people who believed that an education was the best way to get ahead. After the first grade, my mother was always a teacher in my school, and my father was always the principal. It was hard to hide. From what I had seen, I was not sure I wanted to follow their examples. They were fine examples, but knowing a field from every angle destroys the mystique. At the time the Navy's recruiting posters said Join the Navy, and See the World. This slogan removed the warts, and left the mystique. I think that was what I wanted, but I had no interest in actually joining the Navy. I wanted a career with no warts.

In the fall of 1949 during my senior year in high school, the principal called me into his office. I said to myself, "What have I done now?" Until I arrived, I didn't know if I was going to see the principal, or my old man. To my surprise, it was the old man, and he just wanted to talk. He was concerned about paying for college, and asked if I was interested in a college scholarship for training through the Navy Reserve Officers Training Corps (NROTC). He said there would be testing and physical examinations, and a lot of competition. I said I was interested before I knew what I was getting into. It would be a good deal if I could qualify.

Within a month I completed what seemed like 100 pages of application and information forms. The Navy was looking for two thousand men of good character in excellent health who were willing to sign a contract for college training in exchange for service in the Navy. The scholarship portion paid tuition, fees, books, transportation costs, and $50.00 every month for four years of college. Each summer required taking a cruise or other training program as assigned. That amounted to free college plus some spending money, plus one all-expense paid vacation each summer till graduation. My part of the bargain was to take Naval Science classes every year till graduation, then accept a commission as an ensign in the regular Navy. From that point forward, I was to serve at the pleasure of the Navy for a period of three years. It was a dream deal, but difficult to imagine actually getting into such a program.

One of the forms was designed to assist with a background check. It asked for the organizations in which you currently hold or previously held membership. Then it asked if you have had any contact with members of such organizations. Then it provided a list of organizations two pages long and a box to check for each. The only organization for youth in Wakefield was Boy Scouts. It was not listed. The form also asked about traffic violations, truancy, vandalism, arrests, criminal records, and civil lawsuits. At that point I worried about the streetlights I shot with my BB gun in Derby when I was eight years old. Fortunately, my record was squeaky clean. Unofficially if I selected the proper references, I might be able to avoid difficulty with my background check. The forms were all completed, signed, and submitted to the Bureau of Personnel, U.S. Navy Department, Washington, D.C. Then the waiting began.

Two months later I was advised to go to the high school in Concordia, Kansas. It was for psychological testing. The instructions were to get plenty of rest, and prepare for a very long day beginning at 8:00 in the morning. I reported to the high school and was shown to the library where the testing would be held. I was one of 100 students in the room. I tried to calculate the chances of being selected. Subsequently I learned that 40,000 students were considered to fill 2,000 slots. At that rate, other things being equal, five students could be selected from the Concordia group. The testing was grueling, taking 50 minutes of every hour with a ten-minute break. I don't remember ever leaving so many test questions blank in my life. At 5:00 in the evening I was miserable and exhausted, and slept in the car all the way home.

A month later I was told to report to the military headquarters in the Main Post Office Building in Kansas City, Missouri. It was for a physical examination and career interview. Reporting as requested, I filled out more forms, had an interview with two people, and participated with fifty persons in a group medical examination. A military group medical examination is a phenomenon impressed indelibly into memory for a lifetime.

One of the forms was a medical history in which you reported everything you knew you had, or knew a family member had. I reported, among other things, a couple of fractured bones, and supplied the details as requested.

The group medical was initially a record reading session of the medical histories, with individual follow-up of questionable items. After this the doctors in charge held a group physical examination. The instructions were simple. Remove all your clothes, including your shoes, and stand at attention in a straight line, shoulder to shoulder, facing east. All fifty stood at attention, naked as jaybirds, while the doctors looked us up the front, sides, and rear for any visible sign of difficulty. One might call this a gross visual examination, but it could not hold a candle to what followed.

The next instruction was to "bend over and spread-em". I was not sure what em was, so I watched the other guys and did what they did. Up to this time, the notion of mooning one's posterior parts had not been coined. Had I been alone in the bathroom, the experience might have been tolerable. Only my mother had seen this particular exposure before, and that was two decades earlier. There I stood in a room full of 50 naked men, bent over and spreading em. The sight was gruesome. Moon we did. Then we were told to put on our clothes, go home, and forget everything we had seen there that day. Such a sight is difficult to forget.

After a month I received word that my application was complete. I was given alternate status, the highest form of rejection. They thanked me for my participation, and wished me good luck. It was now summer 1950, and time to make final plans for college. My application to the University of Kansas was accepted. I arrived in Lawrence during rush week, a number of days before official registration, and pledged the Sigma Phi Epsilon fraternity. I was ready to start school, but had no idea what kind of major I might select. The NROTC was but a distant memory.

While eating lunch at the fraternity house, I was told I had a message at the Western Union Office. I had no idea what kind of message might be so urgent. It was from the Navy Department, Bureau of Personnel. It said:

BE ADVISED CHANGE FROM ALTERNATE TO REGULAR STATUS NROTC. IF ACCEPT, ADVISE THIS OFFICE, PROCEED IMMEDIATELY OREGON STATE COLLEGE, CORVALLIS AND REPORT PROFESSOR OF NAVAL SCIENCE FOR DUTIES AS ASSIGNED.

I had hit the mother lode! Free college, spending money, paid summer cruise-vacations, plus transportation at government expense. While I had never heard of Oregon State College, it really didn't matter. I packed my bags and returned to Western Kansas to prepare for the long journey to the west coast.

The next seven years of my life were on the Navy's drawing board. I looked forward to the journey with excitement and enthusiasm. I repacked my bags and boarded the Union Pacific's City of St Louis headed west for Portland and Corvallis, wherever they might be.

BEAVER COUNTRY

Oregon was 40 hours from western Kansas by train, a long ride to endure in one shot. The train went straight to Denver, then jogged north to Cheyenne and west. Some of the mountain scenery was beautiful, and helped to break up the long trip. The final leg into Portland along the Columbia River Gorge was one of the more spectacular rides in the country. I knapped in the station in Portland an hour or so, then caught a connecting train into Corvallis. I knew nobody in town. Classes didn't start for several days, so I had time to look around campus, report to the Commanding Officer at the Navy Unit, and find a place to stay during pledge week. Sigma Phi Epsilon had been told of my pledge at Kansas, and included me among their freshman pledge class. It was to be my home for the next two years.

The Sig Ep house was a short two-block walk from north campus, where most of my classes were held. The campus was not large with fewer than 6,000 students. The farthest point on campus from the fraternity was ten minutes on foot. The downtown section was an equally short distance to the east, making it possible to hoof-it anywhere in town. The weather in Corvallis was a complete surprise. Around mid-October, it started to drizzle, not rain but drizzle. I had arrived from the western prairie without any rainwear. In Kansas when it rains you wait till it goes away then continue your business. I waited three months. Then I learned it would probably drizzle until April. Six months of drizzle is a perfect climate for studying, but not much else.

The Sig Eps were a fascinating bunch in a novel house. Unlike the other fraternities, they had no housemother. With their structure they boasted about receiving the national fraternity scholarship award for 21 successive quarters. I was not sure how well I fit with such a group. Dress during the evening meal was formal requiring a coat, dress shirt and tie. Study hours after dinner were strictly enforced. Sixty members and pledges lived in the house with a few more living in local apartments. On drill day all Navy students were required to dress in full uniform. I discovered eight of the brothers were also members of the Navy Unit. Five of the eight were in my pledge class, which helped me feel right at home.

One of the navy pledges, Wayne Annala, asked the house president for a definition of a dress shirt, presumably to make sure he complied with the dinner dress code. At the next evening meal he arrived with his white "dress shirt". It consisted of a collar attached to a left shirt pocket, and two detached cuffs on his wrists. The balance of the shirt under his dinner jacket, not required by definition, was missing, having been cut away with scissors. As one might predict, Wayne became a lawyer, and plied his trade for several decades as the County Attorney in Hood River. By some quirk or skullduggery, Wayne also managed to avoid commissioning in the Navy, and never served a day.

One of the nation's first panty raids was held about a block from the fraternity. Several of the brothers were active participants. This may have been a prelude to tail hook, but the girls appeared to be eager participants in the activities. Panty raids preceded streaking, which peaked in the 1960s. Exactly what all might happen during such a raid is speculative. The apparent climax occurred when some guy would lean out of an upstairs dorm or sorority window waving the girls' underwear, or throw them down to his friends waiting below. All the guys cheered as though they had achieved something of consequence. I had a totally different notion as I watched from outside the sorority. Coming from the great farmland, entering someone's home uninvited is worse than trespassing, and folks have been shot for less. Once inside, to continue into their bedrooms, closets and dressers uninvited is at best a serious invasion of one's privacy. I may be a prude, but I prefer not being shot.

Later in my freshman year one of our members asked me to join him as a houseboy for the Delta Zeta sorority, about a block from our house. Houseboys were primarily mealtime assistants who set the tables, served the food, and waited on the girls' mealtime needs. We worked breakfast, lunch, and dinner. After each meal we cleared the tables, straightened up the dining room, washed the dishes, cleaned up the kitchen, and left. In exchange for this service, we were paid $15.00 a week, plus all the food we could eat. A collateral benefit was the up-close and personal contact with all the sorority girls. Those who were available, interested, and looking, managed to hang around the dining room and kitchen before and after meals. This experience was the triple crown of college life at Oregon State and continued for two exemplary years.

An annual highlight at the fraternity was the Fireman's Ball. It was a spectacular weekend during which the house was totally renovated for a party and dance. The furniture was moved to the perimeter of the rooms. A three-story tailored slide was assembled outside of the house. After two stories of descent outdoors, the slide entered a living room window, merging with the floor. The carpets were removed and the floors were polished like glass. Each guy with his date would walk to the third floor, go through the window and up several more steps to the top of the slide. At the top of the slide they would spread a blanket, select some position for the slide, and let go. At the top was pure acceleration. At the lower end each couple would emerge from the slide onto the floor and swoosh through the living room, hallway, and dining room. With a good slide one could make it through the kitchen door. It was a magnificent ride, and at least one picture was taken of each couple, clad in their pajamas, as they came off the end of the slide into the living room. Some of the pictures were priceless. The slid-ing and dancing continued into the wee-hours of the morning. The below picture shows our first slide as we emerged from the mouth of the dragon. My slight smile and the arms wrapped around my chest are parts of the experience. The expression on my date's face says it all.

The freshman year passed without incident. I changed majors only once, and made grades sufficient to be initiated into the brotherhood. As is characteristic of Corvallis in the spring, the drizzle stopped. With the end of spring quarter, it was time to return to western Kansas, and prepare for my first cruise with the Navy. My orders were to report to the USS Wis-consin, an Iowa class battleship, in Norfolk in three weeks. I was ready.

UNCLE SAM'S TRAVEL

At the end of spring quarter, each Navy student had three weeks to report to his summer training cruise in Norfolk, Virginia. From Oregon that is about 3,000 miles one-way. We were all offered the usual assortment of travel options at government expense. We could request travel vouchers for train or bus transportation, while flying was not an option. The military services used only public transportation or reimbursement for travel by private car when authorized. Minimum cost to the government was a requirement.

As poor students we discussed the many options, and in the process calculated how much we would receive traveling by car. Round trip from Corvallis to Norfolk was about 6,000 miles. Travel reimbursement at 5 cents a mile would be $300 per person. None of us had a car. As we all needed to go, we figured that four in a car would generate $1200. This was all potential money, as we would travel at our own expense, then be reimbursed when the trip was completed. With this sum we could buy a used car, pay the operating costs, and have some spending money left over at the end of the trip. In the business school this was called an economy of scale. It seemed a reasonable plan, so four of us agreed to pursue the adventure. The group included Jim Todd, Jim Grimm, Jack Thomas, and me. We were all in the same pledge class at the Sig Ep house.

Todd offered to look for an appropriate used car. Shortly thereafter he identified a 1939 Plymouth sedan in good condition with high but reasonable mileage. As this was 1951, the car was only 12 years old. For $350 dollars we were in business, and still had $850 remaining. We estimated operating expenses at $100 maximum. If all worked out as planned, we would have $750 left over at the end of the trip to divide among ourselves. In addition, we would still own the car, which we could use, or sell as we saw fit. The plan was set, travel dates established, and we all went home to prepare for our first summer cruise. As I lived in Kansas, I rode the train back home where they were to pick me up in two weeks.

During this era the only interstate highways were a stretch from San Francisco to Los Angeles, and a second from Chicago to New York called the Pennsylvania Turnpike. Most of the other U.S. highways were two-lane roads, which followed the section lines from town to town. A cross-country trip required a lot of city driving with open intersections, stop signs and stoplights. It was a ponderous ordeal for which the Navy said 350 miles a day was enough. Three thousand miles at 40 miles an hour would require 75 hours, a little over three straight days for a one-way trip driving 24 hours a day. Reasonable young persons might figure driving 12 or 15 hours. The group opted to drive continuously, day and night, across the entire country.

An important advantage of this plan was to avoid some of the summer heat. Without air conditioning, the traveling could be miserable during daylight hours. Cars at the time were notorious for running hot when driven steadily at highway speeds, when loaded, or going uphill. We were planning to do all three. Traveling at night provided a break from the heat and avoided the daytime traffic in the towns along the way. The plan also allowed half of the travel to be performed at night when the car would run cooler. With four of us, we could switch drivers as needed.

On departure day the Oregon three left on schedule, and planned to arrive in western Kansas around noon the following day. Their selected route went through eastern Oregon, Idaho and Wyoming. At Cheyenne they leave the mountains behind, and follow the foothills to Denver. Beyond Denver it is all high plains with rolling hills and prairie. I packed my bags in preparation for their timely arrival. At noon they had not arrived. As they were on the road it was not likely they would call. Long distance calls often took as long as the drive for short distances. The only option was to wait. I waited, while visions of doom or major car repairs were rampant.

Six hours later they arrived appearing haggard and worn. Their story was interesting, though not unexpected for a group unfamiliar with roads in the prairie. They had left Oregon early in the morning and had driven all day, changing drivers as needed. Everything was working like a clock. Late that evening they turned south at Cheyenne and drove through Denver toward Limon right on schedule. At Limon they were to make the final highway change onto U.S. 24 into Kansas. It was now 4:00 in the morning. They had been on the road more than a full day. Todd was driving while the other two were sleeping like babies.

Just west of Limon was a modern interchange which merged slowly from one highway to another. Todd took the first turn identified as U.S. 24. He continued driving through towns and countryside until the natives began to stir. Just before dawn he was concerned that the road was particularly hilly, even mountainous. He said to his buddies I didn't know there were mountains in Kansas. They agreed, and stopped to assess the situation. They were on the right highway, U.S. 24, but they were traveling west, and had driven back up into the mountains well beyond Colorado Springs. This side trip in the dark took them 300 miles out of the way and accounted perfectly for the six-hour delay. It was one of the few times that any travelers had seen the Kansas mountains.

The balance of the trip was surprisingly without incident. The car ran perfectly. The weather was tolerable. The group was congenial. We were all reimbursed for travel as expected, and pocketed the extra money as a bonus for our courage. Todd became attached to the car and negotiated to buy our shares for a reasonable price, giving each of us a little added bonus. We figured it was exactly the way Uncle Sam would want us to travel, – haggard and worn.

THE REAL NAVY

We arrived in Norfolk a day early and reported aboard the USS Wisconsin. It was one of four Iowa class battleships built for World War II. It was 900 feet long, 96 feet across, and weighed 64,000 tons. It had a very low profile in the water, possibly because of the 6-armor plate, which surrounds the entire ship below the water line. Three 16" gun turrets with three guns each gave it an ominous appearance. Dual 5" gun turrets surrounded the superstructure, and 50mm quad turrets were attached everywhere. It was clearly designed to throw a lot of metal everywhere in a hurry.

The training cruise was scheduled to last six weeks. For the midshipmen this was our first contact with the real Navy. It was the first time we were required to wear uniforms all day, every day. It was the first time we lived in crew's quarters built for dozens of bodies in each compartment. We were expected to use all the proper terminology, some of which should not be repeated. We were expected to salute officers appropriately. We were expected to report to our muster stations first thing in the morning after breakfast. When your name was called you answered "here". If not, you were late. The rules were clear and simple. We were expected to get the word, know what it meant, and respond accordingly. This was a whole new ballgame compared with living in a fraternity house and attending class at Oregon State. Toto knew we were no longer in Kansas.

Midshipmen were neither fish nor fowl aboard the ship. As a group we must have been a royal pain in the butt. This is not quite the exact Navy terminology for midshipmen, but is as close as is socially appropriate. There was no such thing as socially appropriate aboard ship. Politically correct language had not yet developed. At the time the Navy had females aboard hospital ships only. The real Navy had only real men aboard, with little need to monitor their language. There were no his and hers restrooms, just *heads*, his heads. The absence of females encouraged uncensored banter among the thoroughly horny sailors.

To maintain midshipmen as a visible class, the uniforms were tailored to make them instantly recognizable. We had navy blue, suntan, and white uniforms. The most distinctive marking was on the white hat of first year Midshipmen. It was designed exactly like the enlisted white with the addition of an inch blue stripe around the top edge of the hat. The sailors didn't want midshipmen to compete for the local honeys in port. To fix this they passed the word that those with blue stripes on their hats had VD. It is surprising how fast the word is spread. While wearing a VD hat, like the one below, it is better to smile.

We spent a lot of time at general quarters, during which all hands were at their battle stations. My battle station was in the number two 16 gun turret. This is the same turret that exploded in the 90s, creating a substantial incident for the Navy. The turret itself is huge and had only one outside entry up a lad-

16

der from the main deck. The guns are loaded and fired from the top deck inside the turret. There are two projectile decks immediately below the gun deck, and powder decks below that. The center portion of the projectile decks, and all other decks in the turret, rotate with the guns, leaving the outside storage areas oriented with the ship.

Loading and firing the big guns is quite a process. The projectiles were over six feet tall, 16 in diameter, and weighed 4,000 pounds. Getting each one from the projectile decks to the gun deck required hydraulic lifts and rams for inserting the projectiles into the breach. Then six powder bags were inserted behind the projectile. A triggering device is inserted, and the breach is closed. With a full charge of powder at the proper elevation, each projectile could travel up to 30 miles. The cost of firing one gun one time was the same as the cost of a new Cadillac. On one occasion we fired all nine 16 guns to the starboard side simultaneously. The recoil force on the ship pushed it 100 feet toward the port side from its former track, an impact felt clearly.

Somewhat surprisingly, it is possible to see the projectile immediately after it leaves the gun, and follow its path through the sky, like a small Cadillac hurtling through the air. When all guns fire, it is best to be below decks with earplugs, or far removed from the muzzle of the guns. The picture taken from the bow of the Wisconsin, shows the two forward 16" gun turrets, pointed directly at us with white muzzle covers. Many of the 5" guns may be seen sticking out from the superstructure like the quills of a porcupine.

The shipboard environment was Spartan at best. There was no air conditioning anywhere in the Navy except on the Newport News, a new cruiser with air conditioning in select areas. Sleeping quarters for the crew were all dormitory style compartments with upper and lower bunks and a locker for each bunk. Air circulation came from blowers with vents into each compartment. They were inadequate, unless you happened to have a bunk next to a vent. There were no desks, chairs or other furniture in the living spaces. All areas below the main deck were watertight compartments with access hatches 8 above the deck level. To walk the length of the ship below the main deck required stepping over each hatch opening into or out of each compartment.

Non-working hours aboard ship was spent writing letters, sunbathing, or watching a movie. There was no other entertainment. The fantail on the main deck was huge, and was protected from the wind by movement of the ship. In good weather a movie screen was hoisted into place on the fantail and movies shown in the open air. In the Caribbean the open air was frequently the only comfortable place on the ship. The best space for letter writing was in the mess-hall before and after meals. It was usually full of homesick midshipmen telling their mothers and girlfriends how miserable they had become since the last liberty port.

With 4000 bodies on board, a fair amount of time was spent

standing in line. We stood in line for breakfast, lunch and dinner. We stood in line for the head before and after breakfast. We stood in line at the ships store, the clothing store, and the geedunk store, the Navy equivalent of Dairy Queen. As we had little else to do, it really didn't matter. Being under-way at sea is an amazingly peaceful experience. After a full day of work, it was easy to relax on the ships weather decks and simply watch the ocean go by.

The cruise was not without its casualties. Two midshipmen were killed through freak accidents aboard ship. One walked under an open hatch several levels below the main deck when a piece of plate steel fell through the hatch striking him directly on the head. According to the stories, he never regained consciousness. The second was assigned a battle station above the bridge. This area was a maze of radar installations, radio antennas, rangefinders, and miscellaneous equipment. He became caught among some of the moving equipment, and was crushed in the process. After an incident or two like this, you become far more careful where you walk and what you do.

This cruise first introduced me to the concept of using smoke and mirrors to good advantage. One of my workstations was in an engine room where it was my responsibility to check on *combustion efficiency*. At first this reminded me of a snipe hunt designed for nave midshipmen, and I was holding the sack. The ship was powered by steam turbines in several engine rooms on both the port and starboard sides. Crude oil-fired boilers were used to generate the steam, which ran the turbines that turned the screws to push the ship that Jack built. Through a system of mirrors, it was possible to see the color of the discharge from the ships stacks, which came directly from the boilers. If it was smoking black, the combustion was fuel rich and required a leaner mixture. If the smoke was white the combustion was too lean, and required more fuel. I would report the color of the smoke through the mirrors, and a boilerman would adjust the fuel mixture appropriately. When the mixture was just right, the discharge in the stacks looked like heat rising from the surface of a desert on a hot day. When I did my job right, the boilers produced most efficiently, turning its four screws as fast as they would go on the least amount of fuel. While smoke and mirrors worked beautifully in the Navy, the concept has been badly corrupted throughout mainstream government.

One of the more exciting shipboard experiences was the speed run conducted just prior to returning to Norfolk. One might suspect a ship of this size and vintage would be ponderously slow. The speed run may have been conducted to determine exactly how fast it would actually go. It was probably designed to burn the carbon residue out of the boilers. It required putting all boilers on line and generating maximum RPM from the ships four screws, then sustaining this output for a sufficient period of time. A ship of this size is not a dragster, and may require ten miles at maximum power before it actually achieves top speed. The Wisconsin achieved a speed of 34 nautical miles-per-hour. That converts to well over 50 miles per hour for landlubbers. Motion aboard ship is not apparent until you watch the water. During this speed run, the ships four screws were blowing a rooster-tail of water twice as high as the fantail, – a height of 50 to 60 feet into the air at the stern of the ship. It was an awesome display of brute power, as shown below.

In addition to the speed, there was also a pounding vibration, which continued 45 minutes throughout the speed run. The vibration could be a normal consequence of churning water. It could also be a residual from the unscheduled stop the ship made earlier in the cruise on the New Jersey shore. In retrospect that stop was one of the highlights of the cruise. For a while it appeared that the Wisconsin might become a permanent companion to the Statue of Liberty in New Jersey. It was not to be!

A SLIP IN THE DEEP

The Navy's summer training cruise in 1951 on the battleship Wisconsin included liberty in several ports. We boarded in Norfolk, and were scheduled for liberty in Halifax, Nova Scotia, New York City, and Guantanamo Bay, Cuba, affectionately referred to as Gitmo. Halifax was great as it is a deep-water port, and the ship was able to tie up along the pier next to the downtown area. Gitmo is a U.S. Navy base on the east end of Cuba, with little surrounding civilization. While Castro had not yet acquired power, his bands of supporters were organizing throughout Cuba at the time, and liberty outside the gate was not authorized. Fortunately, we were in Gitmo only for the day where we took on fuel and left. It was in the Big Apple where the Wisconsin almost achieved memorial status. It happened this way:

Like most water traffic, we steamed past Long Island and Brooklyn, then turned north, and moved beyond Wall Street and the Statue of Liberty into the Hudson River. With the assistance of several tugs, the ship was moved into its designated mooring site. The ships bow was secured to a mooring buoy in the middle of the river. As was the custom at the time, the stern of the ship was allowed to swing freely with the tide, the wind, and the river current. When all was secure, the boilers were shut down, and the big girl was put fully to sleep. The port watch was set, and liberty announced.

During this same time period, the deck crew lowered the ladders along the ships sides, and the tenders were used to ferry the crew ashore. The captain's gig was the first into the river. The captain and his senior officers left immediately for liberty. During the next hour a number of LCVPs were lowered for the crew to use on liberty. LCVP stands for landing craft vehicle personnel. They are huge metal bathtub-like structures with diesel power, and are capable of carrying vehicles or personnel. The bow of each is a ramp, which can be lowered to permit rapid loading or unloading. The LCVPs were our liberty boats, and were loaded with dozens of sailors and midshipmen for each trip into the shore. Everything was proceeding exactly as planned.

As it happened, we had entered the harbor and river with the tide. This moderated the effect of the current, and made the mooring process somewhat easier. As the tide started moving out, the river current became stronger, exerting an increased force on the ship's mooring buoy. The port watch was responsible to make sure the ship was secure, and to take appropriate action in the event of a problem. For an hour or longer nothing unusual was apparent. Then it seemed the ship might be moving, but it was difficult to tell as the ship was securely fastened to the buoy. Then someone on the bridge took a fix on one of the waterfront buildings. A few minutes later a second fix confirmed that the building had moved north, or the ship had moved south. How could this possibly be when we were tethered tightly to the mooring buoy?

A few minutes later, it was clear our position had changed once again. Not only was the water moving but the ship was also moving, taking the buoy with us. The force of the current, the tide, and the ship had overcome the huge chunk of concrete anchoring the buoy to the river bottom. As the tide was scheduled to continue going out for several hours, there was no reason to believe the ship would suddenly stop, but would continue moving until some of the forces on the ship changed. It was clearly an emergency situation. Not only were we moving with the current, the bulk of the current's force was on the starboard side of the ship, pushing us toward the New Jersey side of the river. Some emergency measures were needed to prevent the ship from becoming a monument on the New Jersey side of the Hudson River.

The ships boilers were fired in preparation for generating our own power. That process, however, heating water and creating steam, could take up to 30 minutes. Emergency radio calls were sent to all local tugs, and within 15 minutes two tugs had appeared. By the time they arrived and could exert a force sufficient to stop the migration, the Wisconsin had slipped well into the mud on the New Jersey side of the river. As we had gone into the mud stern first, the ships four screws were buried, and would be useless for removing us from this predicament. We came to our final resting place about 50 yards from some old warehouses, almost four city blocks downstream from our original position. With the tugs exerting a constant force against the port side of the ship, the hope was to keep the ship from going deeper into the muddy river bottom.

There is really not much you can do when a 64,000-ton ship requiring water 30 feet deep comes to rest on a muddy river bottom. The long-term plan was to wait until the tide finished going out, then comes back in again. As we were in the river current, there was a serious question about how much influence the tide would have on the level of the water. Hopefully high tide would raise the ship enough to free it from the river bottom, and with the help of tugs, push us back into the channel. High tide was many hours away, with little more to do than wait till that time. This was plan A.

While we were waiting for the tide, I took the following picture. In addition to one of the tugs, a liner similar to the Normandy may be seen in the background. The Normandy was one of the premiere cruise liners of the era, but was destroyed by fire while being converted to a troop ship during the war.

Plan B was not nearly as pretty. New York City was only our second port of call, and the training cruise was just two weeks along, with over four weeks to go. In the event that the tide does not raise the ship enough to free the Wisconsin, the next step is to determine the variation in high tide. As the tide moves with the moon, the absolute highest tide would occur sometime within the next 26 days. That could be a long time to wait for the absolute highest tide to arrive. Had we gone aground at the peak of this period, our chances of getting an additional lift from the tide were slim. Under this plan the Wisconsin could become a permanent memorial on the New Jersey side of the river, competing with the Statue of Liberty for visitors.

Plan B was also an immediate nightmare with 500 midshipmen on board, and no way to continue the training exercises in port. Within a day or two alternate training plans would be required, or the midshipmen would need to be sent home. This, in effect, would terminate the cruise for the summer.

The captain was eventually contacted ashore, and returned to his ship, this time in the mud in New Jersey. He waited, as we all waited, until the tide turned. The tugs continued to push us relentlessly toward the channel. Hours later, the tide actually rose about a foot, which was sufficient to dislodge the hull from the mud. With help from a fleet of tugs by this time, the Wisconsin was pushed clear of the mud, and back into the channel. Her boilers were steaming, and she was ready to move under her own power. Taking no chances, the tugs were retained to accompany the ship to a new and safer location.

As the Hudson River and its mooring buoys had proven to be unreliable, the Captain elected to remove the ship from the Hudson entirely. He selected an anchorage about a mile south of Brooklyn, where he dropped anchors from both the bow and stern of the ship to hold it securely in place. Instead of the Big Apple, Coney Island became the alternate port of call. The ships LCVPs unloaded the liberty parties 50 yards from the amusement park. From the captain's perspective, this was vastly superior to being aground in New Jersey.

With our return to Norfolk, our first summer cruise was over. We packed our bags and headed back across the country to finish what was left of the summer.

THAT SUCKING
SOUND

After being home a few short weeks in the summer of 1951, it was time to return to Oregon State for my sophomore year. With enough bags and boxes to last through the school year, I bid the folks goodbye in Hays and settled into a coach on the Union Pacific's City of St. Louis. We were not out of Kansas when I experienced the first signs of a toothache. It was in a lower molar on the left side of my mouth. As this was my first toothache, I was totally ignorant about what might be done to alleviate the pain. The forty-hour trip to Corvallis was not destined to be a leisurely walk in the park.

As the tooth was in the lower jaw, I made my first startling discovery. The decay was apparently quite substantial, and there was a space between the teeth at the site of the decay. I learned that most of the pain was secondary to saliva, which collected around the tooth. When I parted my lips, and sucked air through the left corner of my mouth, directing as much air as possible through the hole between the teeth, the pain was almost eliminated. The wind sucked the saliva away from the decayed area, and I returned to almost pain-free status for several seconds. This was an exciting initial discovery.

Then I made a second, equally startling discovery. My salivary glands were stuck on maximum output, and produced a flood of fluid on a continuing basis. I would suck the fluid away from the teeth, and my salivary glands would fill the space back up in the next few seconds. I would suck, and it would fill. Suck and fill. Suck and fill. I had become totally obsessed with these chemical, organic, or bodily functions, which were never a part of my conscious state up to that time. I was also painfully aware that this process was destined to continue for the next 35 hours, day and night, until I could get off the train. I was confident the Union Pacific would not stop the train while I visited a dentist. The whole miserable scene was not a pleasant prospect.

While I had never taken a course in chemistry, I became my own test tube, experimenting and recording the results. I was trapped in a process from which I could not extract myself. I concluded that the saliva was a catalyst, which triggered the nerve. Removing the catalyst through a blast of fresh, cool air, had the effect of drying the exposed nerve, and interrupted its message to the brain. Now that I had figured it out, the problem became the myriad of ways to prevent moisture from entering the area. I discovered there are dozens of ways, all of which are temporary. Salivary glands are relentless robot-like workers, and gravity was their co-conspirator in producing my pain. Just what can you do about gravity?

I learned to breathe through my mouth, as the airflow produced a continuous drying effect. It was not as efficient as a forceful sucking, but it prolonged the dry state, delaying the moment required for the next suck. Then I learned that I could use gravity for my own purposes, by cocking my head to the right. This diverted the saliva to the right side of my mouth, leaving the left in a drier state. I learned to lie down on my right side for the same reason. This combination of influences, sucking, breathing through my mouth, and tilting my head to the right allowed me to endure several minutes without sucking. This process of experimentation went on for several hours.

It was at about this point that I became aware of the other people on the train. There were not many, but they seemed to believe that I had a chronic tic, mannerism, or other aberration. They were right. They tried to figure out exactly why I was sucking and tilting my head to the right. They would glance at me, but as soon as I would suck, or tilt, they would look away. There were clearly social consequences from my dilemma. For them, it was the sucking and tilting that called attention to my plight. To minimize this influence, I wanted to suck as little as possible and tilt as little as possible, yet when the pain achieved a certain level, I had to suck again. When they thought I was not looking, they would glance back at me.

My next discovery was that acute conditions, like a toothache, tend to become chronic. What works initially loses its effectiveness, and the acute discomfort returns. I found that I needed to suck harder, and more often. That sucking sound became a pervasive quality of that specific train car, and I was the one doing the sucking. I sucked, and sucked. Every few seconds I sucked. One at a time, the folks on the car migrated to other cars on the train, leaving me to suck and tilt without an audience. At each stop, new folks would settle into the car, and shortly thereafter I would hear someone say, "What's that sucking sound?" Then they would locate the sound and the curiosity would begin again. As soon as they saw the head tilting with the sucking, they would gather up their things, and move to another car. It was fine with me, as I could then suck and tilt in peace as needed for pain.

Throughout this trip I reviewed why this might have occurred. My dental history was unusual, as I had never previously had a cavity in any tooth. I had arrived in Corvallis a year earlier with perfect teeth, crooked lowers, but perfect. The first year as a student was spent in the fraternity basement, which included a recreation area with couches, chairs, a ping-pong table, and a Coke machine. That was where I did most of my studying. That was where I drank several Cokes every day. I calculated that I had consumed nearly 1000 regular Cokes during my first year at Oregon State. Coke machines at the time dispensed one beverage, in a bottle. I was living on regular Coca Cola, complete with sugar, six ounces at a time. It was not just the drink of choice, it was the only drink dispensed from the machine. It cost a nickel. I had bathed my mouth in nickel Coke for nine months.

I arrived in Corvallis during regular working hours, and checked immediately into a dentist's office. He said the molar was in an advanced state of decay, and could not be salvaged. He pulled it, root and all. Then he examined the rest of my teeth. He said that 13 additional cavities were all in need of immediate attention. Over the next several weeks, I spent more time in the dentist's chair than in my entire life prior to that time. In those days, pain-killers had not yet been developed for dentists, requiring that I spend another dozen hours' of pain in the dentist's chair. His bill was several hundred dollars, an amount equal to ten times that spent on coke the previous year. My conclusion was inevitable. For every nickel I spent on coke, I would spend another 50 cents at the dentist's office, and another minute of pain in his chair. The cumulative effect was a miserable payoff for quenching your thirst.

That 40-hour train ride was the longest seven days of my life, but the sucking and tilting was finally over.

NAVY WATCH BUSINESS

The cruise on the Wisconsin gave me a crystal-clear picture of my career choices in the Navy. It was not pretty. What few decisions I had made were to avoid sorry circumstances, rather than to do something I enjoyed. Maybe that is the way such choices are supposed to be made, but it didn't seem right at the time. This is the way it happened to me.

Bow View, Battleship USS Wisconsin

One of my regular duties on the Wisconsin was standing watch. On a ship of this size, hundreds are standing watch all the time, 24 hours a day. The best example of a watch was from the old sailing movies. The only guy standing an actual watch in these movies was the little guy who would crawl 100 feet up a rope ladder into the crow's nest at the top of the mainmast. Up there he would get out his spyglass and scan the horizon looking for land, or enemy ships, or shoals and reefs, or ladies in bikinis, not necessarily in that order. Whenever something happened, he was sitting in the catbird seat, and would shout down whatever was happening to whoever was listening. His watches were scripted, and always created quite a stir.

What the movies did not show was what he did when nothing exciting was happening, because it didn't make a very good movie. He was still in the crow's nest with his spyglass looking for things that weren't there. Throughout his watch, he looked, and looked, and looked, and never had anything to shout about. After four hours he would crawl out of the crow's nest, and back down the rope ladder. He was hungry, frozen, and exhausted. He didn't know what to do first, get warm, eat, or sleep. So, he got a bowl of gruel and ate it in the rack.

This deals only with the actual watch itself. What is not scripted is that watches occur at all hours of the day or night, on a relentless schedule. You don't make up the schedule! You check the watch list, which is posted in the duty area, to see when its your turn. To fully experience watches, you really have to lay them end-to-end. You probably have an assigned duty station and explicit duties while there. There is a duty log in which you record everything noteworthy that happens at that duty station during your watch. A watch on the bridge, for instance, will include the captain's orders. It specifies that the ship must make a course change at 0300 in the morning.

With your watch from 12 to 4, you have nothing in particular to do for the first three hours. What you actually do is look forward to the course change, the only thing you have to do for four hours. At precisely 3:00 in the morning, you execute the course change. It says come right to course 120 true. As soon as the ship is steady on course 120, your excitement is over. That takes a few minutes. You record at 0300 came right to course 120 true in the log book. At 0315 you are bored out of your gourd, so you make another entry in the log. 0315 steady on course 120 true. Then you have another 45 minutes to spend on watch waiting for something to happen. It never does.

On the bridge at sea in the peacetime Navy, it is customary to steam in a straight line. It is entirely possible to stand watches for several straight days. Every day there are six watches, two of which are yours steaming in a straight line. It is like driving through Kansas on Interstate 70, except the scenery never changes. There are no course changes to enliven your day. You spend days waiting for something to happen. The example of a watch with a course change is a reasonably exciting example, which otherwise reverts to a standard watch, when nothing happens at all.

In the old days there were sailors standing duty all over the ship. There was the one on the wheel, struggling against the wind and the rain. There were those on the sail crew, fighting to raise, or lower the sails. There were those in the bilges rowing the oars. For the crew on the oars, there was a crew chief with a loudspeaker saying Pull ... Pull ... Pull ... Pull you landlubbers, or you won't get your daily ration of gruel. Each of these sailors was performing an essential task. It was no different in the modern Navy.

Standing watch was in the same class as watching paint dry. It dried whether I was watching or not. I preferred not watching, particularly at 0300 in the morning. I wanted something to happen, something to do. I needed a project to keep me awake.

One of the key problems with watches was dealing with the consequences. They were numerous. One consequence, as illustrated in the old movies, was the punishment when caught sleeping on watch. From my perspective, any red-blooded American sailor should sleep on watch, as that was the most rational thing to do. The Navy doesn't agree with this position, and specifies punishment for violators at the captain's discretion. In the old days, a favorite punishment was keel-hauling. This required tying the offender's hands and feet with different ropes. Then they would pass one rope under the ship, without saying exactly how they got the rope under the ship. Then they would pull the violator through the water under the ship holding both ends of the rope. The problem here, which may be self-evident, is when the rope pullers are not well coordinated, and end-up pulling on both ends. This is both cruel and unusual if the violator is underwater at the time. On the Wisconsin, it was 150 feet across the beam with 30 feet of draft on each side. That is a total of 210 feet at the end of a rope, all underwater, not counting the barnacles. The best advice was to stay awake while on watch.

A four-hour watch is not really an adequate daily work schedule, so most schedules were four hours on and eight hours off, four more hours on and eight more off. That is two watches a day, one during the day, and another during the night. The full impact of watches was experienced only after enduring such a schedule for several days. It seemed like a form of sickness to actually choose this kind of career as a line of work. I really needed something quite different.

Not all watches were four-hours in length. The sailors pictured above are engaged in a Deck Division duty called holystoning. It is a regular duty, or punishment, during eight daylight hours. Because all weather decks on the ship are made of wood, they required constant care. As you may see, seven sailors and one midshipman are in line, each with a stick. The stick is inserted into the shallow hole in the top of each stone. To be sure every board is smoothed by stoning, these eight sailors stand in a straight line working each board simultan-eously. It must be performed in perfect unison, like rowing a slave galley, or else the stones break and a brawl ensues. Given the size of the ship, if this is your watch, you can finish the entire ship in several days. Then you may start over again. This is one way to avoid night watches.

I had no problem with working, but watch schedules re-quired working twice a day, day and night, forever. Watches were hours of boredom separated by a few moments actually doing something useful. I discovered, to my amazement, that the people performing these watches were all known as line officers, and could be identified by a small star worn on their uniforms. They should all have large stars for courage and per-sistence in the face of boredom. Then I learned about the other kinds of officers called staff officers. I decided that whatever staff officers did, that was what I wanted to do. The solution was readily available, and little did I know that I had already made the proper decision for my prospective career in the Navy.

During my freshman year, I switched from engineering to the business school. Running the Navy's business was much more to my liking, and would get me out of the watch business, a pure form of monkey business.

Shortly after returning to Oregon State for my sophomore year, I conferred with my Navy advisor about changing to the Supply Corp, the Navy's business division. My first application was deemed frivolous, and was turned down somewhere in the chain of command. I never knew where the chain was broken, but the request probably never left the campus. Oregon State did not have a Supply Corps program, which was available only at selected schools.

I appealed the decision, and in the process called upon some outside help with the decision in Washington. With this help, the initials P.I. (political influence) were stamped in large let-ters on the outside of my service record. I had heard that most of the Navy folks didn't pay any attention to P.I., so there was no problem using it, if you had it. Then there were the others who were incensed over outsiders who messed with the Navy's internal decisions. These other folks had a second acronym they stamped in large letters on the outside of your record. Those initials were P.O., and we all know what that stands for. You don't want these other folks writing the orders for your next duty station. You could spend the next three years under the North Pole. I knew in advance I was not interested in that part of the Navy.

Voila! The request was approved. I finished my second year at Oregon State. I knew I would miss the girls at the Delta Zeta sorority. I was their houseboy for two years, serving all their needs as they arose. It was a sad affair kissing them all goodbye. I bid farewell to the fraternity brothers, and returned home. The following year I entered the Supply Corps Training Program at the University of Kansas. The watch business was finally over, and I started looking forward to a watch worth shouting about. Or at least, so it might seem!

WILD BLUE YONDER

Saying a final goodbye to Oregon State and Corvallis in June 1952, I returned home to Kansas for three short weeks. This summer training program was designed as a recruiting opportunity for two of the Navy's special forces. All second-year midshipmen were ordered to converge on the Naval Air Station (NAS) Corpus Christi, Texas, for an introduction to the wild blue yonder. After three weeks in Corpus Christi, we were to go to Little Creek, Virginia, for an introduction to the Marines. How many recruits were enticed into these special forces is anybody's guess, but it was a fascinating, all-expense paid vacation from my perspective. I had only recently made the decision to serve in the Navy's Supply Corps, a specialization which extracted me from all deck watches, both underway and in port.

The Navy was looking for pilots for both single and multi-engine planes. The first three weeks at the Corpus NAS was fully scripted, and was designed to impress all the midshipmen with the attractive benefits of flying. It was an outstanding orientation to flying at the time, and was far more comprehensive than the Navy really intended. Most midshipmen and most civilians at the time had never flown in an airplane. I was probably an exception as I had flown commercially, and had endured one hair-raising experience in a private plane. This background conditioned me to assess the risks associated with flying, rather than the benefits which might accrue. I was a skeptic from the outset.

Initially we were selected into groups of 20 for a flight in a Martin Mariner, or PBM. It was the Navy's utility flying boat, patrol aircraft, and the first transport which could operate from both water and land with equal facility. The Martin was powered by two Wright engines, and flew well below its top speed of 200 mph. I would guess this top speed was achieved only in a dive, and dives were not recommended for such a plane. With its fuel carrying capacity, the PBM was capable of staying aloft for days at a time. Because of the speed and distances involved in its missions, more than one pilot was often required. They spent most of their time on such missions sitting in the air, watching and waiting. This was the routine hour after hour.

As soon as it was our turn to go up, we took off from the airstrip, and went on a routine over-water flight for about two hours. Each of us was given a turn at the controls. As an experience, it was like driving a freight train on the straight and level with gentle corners that required a mile to complete 90 degrees. From 3000 feet at a reasonably slow speed, it was necessary to find a fixed object on the ground to confirm that you were actually moving, as any experience of motion was missing, unlike a freight train. This was our experience with multi-engine aircraft.

Our introduction to single engine planes included individual instruction in the Navy's Basic Instrument Trainer, the AT-6, also known as the SNJ. My introduction was an eye-opener. Each of the midshipmen was paired-off with a pilot to begin the session. We were issued flight gear, which consisted of coveralls and a headset. After suiting up, we were assigned our individual aircraft, which we then had to locate among hundreds on the field. Our assigned plane was #36. As these planes were first built for the Navy in the 30s, this particular plane was one of the earliest of the original models. A nicely restored version is shown below.

We finally found the plane, climbed aboard, strapped in, plugged in the headphones, and checked our internal communications. Fortunately, the phones worked fine. The pilot took the front seat, and I climbed into the rear. My first discovery was that the runway was out of sight when seated and buckled in. It is apparently necessary to fly blind until something happens to change your view. During takeoffs, as soon as the tail lifts off the runway, the runway then becomes visible from both the front and the rear seats. As the plane is a tail-dragger, it also has a tendency to turn sideways at touchdown, requiring corrective pressure on the appropriate foot-pedal.

There are few experiences comparable to the noise created by a single radial engine, particularly when the engine is mounted directly in front of you. The vibration is substantial, but the noise is deafening, and is un-muffled, as muffling reduces the engines power output. The exhaust is simply vented away from the front of the plane, with little noise suppression. Because of the noise, great headsets firmly planted over both ears were required for any person-to-person communication in the plane. If it works, you are in business. If it does not work, you are deaf and mute, and must rely on sign language. A great deal of noise still filtered through the headset, turning all communication into a problem.

We taxied from the flight line onto the taxiway, and were in a long line of SNJs approaching the end of the runway. When we were one or two planes from takeoff, I became alarmed that the air in the rear cockpit seemed to be cloudy, if not smoky. I asked the pilot if he smelled or saw any smoke. As soon as he understood the question, he turned around and looked back at me through what was then a cloud of smoke. He had no idea what might be happening, but confirmed that he, too, saw the smoke. He suggested that we must have a little electrical problem with either burning wires or radio equipment. He taxied out of line immediately, radioed the tower that we were returning with some unknown kind of smoke problem in the cockpit, and were shutting the radio equipment off. Then he opened the canopy to blow out the smoke and bring in some fresh air. We taxied into a safe area of the field, and crawled out of the plane pronto. The pilot figured as soon as we shut the system down, the problem might go away. I don't know if the problem disappeared, but we were clear of the plane well before the fire truck arrived.

To that point, I had survived running out of gas at 600 feet in a Funk, requiring an emergency landing in a plowed field. The next flight produced a fire in the cockpit, one of the more dreaded consequences of flying in airplanes. I was not particularly excited about crawling into another SNJ. The pilot, on the other hand, appeared to be totally unconcerned, as though this kind of event was just part of the routine. While waiting for another plane to be assigned, he asked if I was interested in some aerobatics. I was aware of a few maneuvers, and suggested that he should help himself to whatever he was comfortable with. I was actually quite uncomfortable with the suggestion, but my ego got in the way, and injected the response for me before I came to my senses.

We received our replacement SNJ, checked it out, taxied to the runway, and took off without incident. We climbed steadily for the next 10 minutes. The pilot asked if I had ever experienced zero Gs. I said I had not, so when we arrived at 8000 feet, he pulled the nose of the plane up another 20 degrees to create a stall. I knew that at some point we would lose our airfoil, the plane would then become a rock, and we would free-fall toward the earth. It happened precisely that way. We lost headway, the right wing fell precipitously, and we fell back toward the tail.

Then as the nose of the plane started for the ground, we began whirling like a corkscrew. The entire world was spinning round and round, and we were seemingly out of control for several complete revolutions.

I asked the pilot if everything was OK. I received no response. Then I asked again, and again received no response. After what seemed like an eternity, he replied that he must have blacked out for a short time. I never knew if he was playing games, testing my reaction, or telling the truth. I suspected he was telling the truth, and was relieved to return to the ground in one piece. My tolerance for planes at that point had been reached, but our orientation to Navy flying was not yet complete.

These flights were all leading up to the grand finale, an air show of the Navy's finest flying demonstrations. On the last full day in Corpus, the orders were issued for full dress uniforms, and assembly of all midshipmen along the waterfront. Our several divisions were marched into formation and placed at ease about 50 feet from the water. From this position we witnessed a PBM taking off from the water using jet assisted take off. It was, of course, like nothing we had experienced. Small rockets had been fixed onto either side of the fuselage of the plane just forward of the tail section. The plane taxied onto its final take-off path, got up onto its step on its own, then fired both rockets simultaneously. At that moment, the PBM, normally an albatross, rose almost instantly into the air and started climbing at an unbelievable rate of ascent. It was an exciting demonstration of a way to use short runways or limited waterways with heavy loads. It is best not to ask about the cost of two disposable rockets.

Immediately after this demonstration, two blue jets buzzed the harbor from the west immediately above the midshipmen. They were moving at an incredible rate of speed, 500 feet above the ground, performing barrel rolls, and streaming red and blue smoke from the wingtips. This was the standard opening for the Navy's Blue Angels, their precision formation flying team, which had performed at air shows all over the country. Advance billing stated with considerable pride that they had never experienced an accident, in spite of their close formation and tight maneuvers. Our attention was directed to the west again, so we would not miss any of the action.

Close formation consists of four planes flying in a diamond configuration. The lead plane has one plane following each wingtip, and the fourth plane flies between these two planes in the rear slot, completing the diamond. In such a formation the wingtips of the lead plane become the orientation point for the planes on the sides, while the tail of the lead plane is the orientation point for the man in the slot position. The slot man's plane may be only a few feet from the tail assembly of the lead plane. This formation is then maintained through straight flight, slow rolls, loops, and other synchronized maneuvers.

With our attention directed to the west, we could see this formation approaching from the horizon. The planes arrived well before the sound of their jets as they started their first pass in a tight formation a thousand feet above the harbor, almost directly over the midshipmen. Just prior to passing, some miscalculation in the formation was apparent. The plane flying in the slot of the formation came up underneath the tail assembly of the lead plane, striking it with enough force to destroy the surface surrounding the air intake. After that the force of the airflow disintegrated the plane from the nose back, ripping what seemed like hundreds of pieces of metal off the plane immediately. This cloud of metal was hurtling toward the ground off shore. I worried about stray pieces landing along the tarmac in front of the midshipmen. In an automatic response, I broke from ranks and ran toward the shelter of the planes outside of the hangars behind us, the most rational thing to do.

What was left of the plane in the slot crashed into the harbor a quarter of a mile beyond us. Some claimed the pilot had ejected just prior to hitting the water, but no parachute was ever visible. It was a moot point at best, as the plane and all related components were traveling well over 500 miles an hour at the time. Impact with any object at that speed was not survivable. Two thousand midshipmen had all witnessed the Blue Angels first fatal accident, and they had done so up close and personal. It was a chilling introduction to flying the Navy's premier jet fighter.

The lead pilot in the formation knew he had been hit, and immediately pulled his plane into a vertical climb. At a high altitude he checked the planes controls to assess the damage to its air worthiness. Reports and rumors indicated that his planes controls became mushy below 200 miles an hour. He requested permission to land at an airstrip near Kings Ranch, where there was a 10,000-foot runway available. He landed without further incident.

Following this brutal introduction to Navy Air, most of us were eager to look at the Marines for its career potential. Exactly how many recruits were obtained for flight training is not known, but the experience might not dent the armor of those died-in-the-wool prospects for pilot training. It might even enhance the challenge of the Navy's Air Corps. The following day we packed our bags and were bussed to the nearest train station for transfer to Little Creek. Our introduction to flying in the navy was far more comprehensive than planned, and clearly revealed the wild blue yonder.

THE MARINE AFFAIR

The train we boarded for Little Creek was a local.   Under contract to transport military personnel, it carried the lowest form of rail priority. With this priority, we moved onto the siding to allow freight trains to pass. With 500 midshipmen aboard, the trip across Texas, Louisiana, Mississippi, Alabama, Georgia, South Carolina, North Carolina, and Virginia consumed over two days. As we had nothing better to do, these 48 hours became an orgy of drinking, card playing, and reliving the hair-raising experiences at the Naval Air Station in Corpus Christi. Following these two very long days, we arrived in Little Creek exhausted, but ready for the games we knew the Marines would expect us to play.

Little Creek was the Marine headquarters for training in amphibious landings. We were issued a complete set of khaki uniforms for making us look like marines. We were then assigned to Quonset huts for living accommodations, and advised to prepare ourselves for a full-scale amphibious landing within a few days. A fleet of ships and landing craft had been assembled for our invasion, which was to emulate the real thing as closely as possible. We were issued M1 rifles, drilled in their assembly and disassembly, and instructed in their use. Then we were taken to the firing range where we practiced firing at an assortment of targets.

As our invasion was to be staged from the sea, we were all assigned to individual ships. The ships included a troop transport, a landing ship tank, and dozens of smaller vessels. As we were now marines, we had little to do with operating the vessels. We were simply passengers as men, equipment, and supplies needed to capture and maintain a beachhead in hostile territory, – a remote stretch of beach south of Little Creek.

I was assigned to the troop transport, which was to carry the first and second waves of assault forces. The troop ship looked like a liberty ship built by the hundreds during the war. Its sleeping compartments were huge areas with bunk beds stacked up to seven levels high, requiring a certain amount of climbing ability and some care to reach the top bunk safely. One such compartment would hold several hundred bodies. You can imagine the sound effects at night from several hundred men trying to sleep in the same compartment. Next you should imagine the same compartment on a hot day with no air conditioning, and virtually no ventilation. The living conditions were miserable for the troops being transported, but vastly superior to sleeping in trenches.

With hundreds of troops on board, all the facilities were stressed beyond a reasonable capacity. A large number of midshipmen never slept in their bunks, but found it far more comfortable sleeping on deck under the moon with a breeze. On arising in the morning, the first chore was to stand in line for the head and related bathroom facilities. Then we stood in line for breakfast, ate breakfast, and left the mess hall. Lunch and dinner followed the same routine. Meals were served on a continuous basis, as the mess hall was small, and there was little else to do. The majority of the first day was spent standing in line. War must have been hell. The consolation was that these circumstances were better then what might follow.

The second day was the amphibious exercise. As with all exercises, they must always begin well before dawn. We were awakened at 3:00 in the morning, and instructed to prepare for our assault. During the evening, the LSD had unloaded dozens of LCVPs for transporting us from the troop ship to the beach. It all happened just like you see it in the documentaries of WWII.

The LCVPs circled by the ship until it was time to load the troops, then they came alongside one by one and took on a full load of troops and equipment. As soon as they were all loaded, they formed a straight line and moved toward the beach so as to arrive simultaneously. It all went without a hitch from the troop ship.

As with the former cruise, not all participants survived the training experience. One midshipman was killed when he jumped off a pontoon as it was moving toward the beach. He jumped into the water before it was fully beached. The list of fatalities is now up to four from two training cruises as follows: USS Wisconsin (2), NAS Corpus Christi (1), and Little Creek Marine Base (1).

The Marines were successful in recruiting one classmate, fraternity brother, and travel companion into the Corps. Jim Todd had an aversion to ships or water, or other things in the regular Navy. He affiliated with the Marines and was commissioned into the Corps on graduation from Oregon State. At one point, Jim had boasted that he had slipped through the stringent Navy swimming qualification examination without taking and passing the test. This may have been his incentive to avoid the Navy. Shortly after his entry onto active duty, he was engaged in another amphibious exercise off San Diego. According to the stories, his landing craft was swamped in the exercise. He did not survive the ordeal. Jim is shown below, decked-out in Marine Khaki in front of our Quonset hut in Little Creek. The stain is compliments of Kodak.

Bob Settles

CRUSTY SHELLBACK

For all landlubbers everywhere, ignorance is no excuse. A crusty shellback is what you become after a grueling initiation into the Ancient Order of the Deep, the hallowed and exclusive realm of King Neptunus Rex, who we will call Rex for short. This exclusive club is not open to just anybody, but is conferred only upon those who fully satisfy the requirements of membership. At a minimum one must cross the equator aboard a navy ship, and you must survive the initiation. This is not an exercise for the faint-hearted, and you are not offered a breather complete with tea and crumpets in route to membership. Those who resist may be marked for life!!!! All new initiates are marked at least until after their first shower.

Knowing the landlubbers among you may not fully appreciate the circumstances, I will offer a brief picture of one quite lethal perspective. The battleship Missouri (BB-63) on which I was initiated in 1953, was manned by over two thousand battle-hardened sailors, a hearty bunch including hundreds who survived the big one, WWII. In spite of their honor and dedication to the real navy, they tend to harbor a cluster of resentments of those in authority. During a summer cruise on which their territory is invaded by hundreds of future navy officers, particularly those lolling on college campuses, an officially sanctioned opportunity to administer a humble pill is the rare opportunity of a lifetime.

And on a ship the size of the Missouri, the weapons of torture are devious and diverse. The initiation ceremony is planned and executed by those who have been through the mill, and who bear the scars from their own searing experience. In the 1950s the navy was still a pure breed, as only Spartacus and Hercules types were assigned to duty on fighting vessels. The only female in sight was the ship herself, which was manned strictly by men. Had women been aboard at the time, there are undoubtedly certain maneuvers during initiation that would have been barred, or preferred as the case may be.

Resurrecting graphic details from the ordeal, the following pictures are offered in order as follows:

1. Meet the royhal couort, and kiss the Royal Baby's belly, smeared with alum and bilge water.

2. Sit on the chair for emersion into the reverse dunking pool.

3. Run the gauntlet with 3" fire hoses swatting at anything that shows.

4. Watch the royal baby as he and the royal court depart.

While a nearby cook picks his nose, many new Crusty Shell-backs are grateful they were not required to kiss the royal behind. That part comes later.

Jim Burgess X

Author, - A Crusty Shellback

TIN CAN SAILORS

Looking back at serving on both the USS Wisconsin (BB-64) and the USS Missouri (BB-63) provides a unique perspective. These two behemoths were among the ships assigned to summer training cruises for NROTC midshipmen in the summers of 1951 and 1953 respectively. Sailing out of Norfolk, the 1951 Wisconsin cruise visited Halifax, Guantanamo Bay, Colon, and New York City, – where she managed to drag her mooring buoy ashore in New Jersey. She was simply too much for the buoy's concrete anchor and the heavy downstream current with approaching low tide.

The 1953 cruise on the Missouri crossed the equator, the occasion for a magnificent initiation ceremony into Neptunis Rex' Ancient Order of the Deep. While steaming toward Rio's anchorage, we encountered some ground swells that produced a series of rolls in excess of 45 degrees. This provides something of a thrill when seated on the back of a dinosaur.

The ride we experienced on the battleships was insignificant when compared with that of the Tin Can Sailors. Exactly where or when the term Tin Can Sailor originated is unknown. What may be inferred is that the very fast, mobile, and much smaller ships known as destroyers (DD) and destroyer escorts (DE) when afloat in a large ocean, resemble tin cans afloat almost anywhere, but in a stormy sea the ride is awesome. They bob and weave and pitch and yaw and splash and wallow in the water as if they were really cans.

On our return trip from Brazil to Norfolk, the tin cans would often come alongside for refueling or re-provisioning, or both. The exercise included firing lines from one ship to another, then hauling successively larger lines across the open water until the means for transporting goods or fuel was sufficient. This meant cargo nets for supplies, or a four-inch hose for fuel. With two ships underway in heavy seas, this operation is performed with great caution.

On one occasion, the destroyer escort USS Tabberer (DE-418) came alongside for refueling. The seas were substantial, and to establish a steady platform for transfer, both ships headed directly into the approaching waves. Because transferring thousands of gallons of fuel requires a period of time, there was ample opportunity to observe the Tabberer as she labored into the heavy seas. The following pictures show the Tabberer with her Bow Up and Bow Down, while transferring fuel. One should take special note of the troops mustered along the starboard side of the forward 5″ gun turret. The ride into and out of the waves from this vantage point can provide an exhilarating and enhanced view, – for a moment. Then comes the fall!

Bow high and dry

Note the fuel line attached. Note as well the sailors, probably midshipmen, mustered on the main deck as they rise precipitously to observe the operation. Finally note the keel portion of the bow 3-5 feet above the trough of the wave. Ride-em cowboy, but hold on with both hands.

Bow down

Whatever goes up comes down. Except for the first picture, few would guess this picture is the Tabberer still taking on fuel, while the five-inch turret and a division of sailors are unexpectedly taking on salt water like drowned rats, totally out of sight. The bow splash is level with the overhead in the conning tower, the Tabberer's first structure directly astern.

It is with a little envy that the battleships were incapable of providing the same level of thrilling ride as that offered all the Tin Can Sailors. "Toto! I don't think we are in Kansas anymore."

THE CONTRACT

Having been raised in the old-fashioned tradition, I believed that a deal is a deal. You are supposed to live up to your deals through thick or thin, richer or poorer, for better or worse. Deals are frequently stated in plain words like I will if you will, or I will, but you have to go first, or I will, but it will cost you fifty bucks. These clearly stated deals are all fine, of course, until it is your turn to keep your end of the deal. That is exactly where I found myself.

There are, of course, different kinds of deals. In the business school, deals are called contracts. They may be written or verbal. If you end-up in court, it is better to have it in writing because people lie. They can go back on their word and lie about the deals they really made. In this case a deal is a deal, – maybe. Under oath they call this perjury, a serious offense for which many persons have gone to jail, excluding recent presidents, of course. The Navy solved this problem for me by requiring a written contract.

On accepting the Navy's offer to pay for my education through four years of college, they required me to sign a contract. Like all contracts, it was several pages of small print. You sign that you have read and understand all the provisions of the contract. I suspect that few persons actually read the many pages of fine print, written by lawyers in language several levels short of plain English. After reading a paragraph or two, any reasonable person starts mumbling to himself. Then it becomes automatic to find the signature line, sign your name, and move on to something more palatable. I did, but I really knew the provisions.

One of the small print provisions stated that I agreed not to get married, I assumed, while attending college. When I was offered the contract, I was only 18 years old. I had met dozens of great marriage prospects, but had not narrowed the field appreciably, as I knew there were dozens more I had not met. I signed the agreement in good faith, believing it was not a big deal. I did not fully appreciate exactly how long four years was, particularly during these more virile years.

In the summer of 1952, fate struck a fatal blow to my deal when I met Lois, a little farm girl from western Kansas. On our second date, I played her sweet ukulele music on a sand bar in the Solomon River. Then I told her we would be getting married in the foreseeable future. She might have asked to go home immediately, but she didn't. The rest is history.

Over the next few months, in view of the Navy contract, we discussed the options. There were only two, and neither was very pretty. We could marry after graduation two years away, or we could marry in secret and risk being caught. The latter, of course, was a breach of contract, and defines our dilemma. Numerous stories were circulating about Navy students who married, none of which could be verified. One student, presumably, was caught, and was asked to leave the program immediately, in effect terminating the contract, college support, and commissioning. A second reportedly went directly to the Commanding Officer, and announced his recent marriage in an apparent attempt to void his contract. The CO stood up, shook his hand, said Congratulations, and asked if he had any other information for him. Presumably the contracts marriage provision was simply ignored. Faced with these conflicting stories, a carefully crafted plan was needed.

I had no interest in voiding the contract, and fully intended to complete training, and serve my three years with a regular commission. At the same time, it seemed arbitrary to void a contract for a circumstance, which bore no relevance to performance under the contract. With this justification, we planned a wedding for the summer of 1953 between my junior and senior years. Secrecy was the keyword, and every effort was focused on keeping it that way. There were to be no announcements and no written invitations. The wedding party was to consist of a maid of honor, a best man, a preacher, and select family members we knew to be trustworthy. The family members were pledged to complete secrecy, trusting nobody.

Because of the risk of official public announcements, like issuance of a license, the wedding was planned for Colorado, rather than Kansas. We felt the greatest risk of discovery would be where we lived every day. For this reason, we chose to live in Topeka, rather than Lawrence, a 50-mile daily commute to the Kansas University campus. The plans were followed explicitly. We married on August 15, 1953 in Allenspark, Colorado, a remote mountain village an hour from Boulder. We moved into an apartment in Topeka, and with the beginning of fall semester I assumed all my usual student activities, while Lois started teaching school in Highland Park. The happy couple is shown in front of the fireplace in Settles cabin in Allenspark.

We had double dated with another Navy student and his fiancé the previous year. Believing they were totally safe, we told them that we had married in August. Following our example, they also got married within a month. Continuing to follow our example, they got an apartment in Topeka, and he and I commuted to Lawrence together for the rest of the year. At the time, there was a continuous gas war in Lawrence and Topeka. We not only shared the cost of commuting, we did so on gasoline for 13 cents a gallon. The daily cost of gas was about a quarter a day each for the 50-mile trip, a bargain by any standard.

Everything was proceeding nicely toward graduation. We knew that at some point, someone would discover our deception. At the time, both sets of parents lived in Palco, a small town off the beaten path in Western Kansas. Any secret in Palco has a half-life of 24 hours. The next day, half the folks in town know the secret. As luck would have it, one of the towns greatest gossips visited in our part of Topeka. She had a friend with a child who attended Lois' school in Highland Park. She asked her friend if there was a Lois Steeples teaching in the school. After a short delay, the friend said the only Lois in school was a Lois Settles. The cat was out of the bag, and was in the hands of Palco's biggest gossip.

At the time, the foremost suspicion about secret marriages was that they were have-to deals. The young lady is pregnant, of course, and the parents might not even know. As everyone in Palco knew both sets of parents, it was prime gossip, and the woman could hardly wait to return to the small town to share her information. Our fathers were both school principals, and were well respected, enhancing the value of the information. For whatever reason, the gossip went first to Lois mother, apparently to validate the information, and find out what was really going on. Did you know that Lois was teaching in Highland Park as Lois Settles? she said. Were they living together? and Is she pregnant? were her additional questions. The last question was the only one of vital interest.

Lois mother was somewhat startled by the questions, but took the honest approach with the woman, who otherwise might look for answers elsewhere. Of course, we know they are married. No, Lois is not pregnant. she said. Then she confided with the woman about the Navy Contract, and the importance of maintaining complete silence. Apparently, the woman was satisfied, and kept the gossip to herself for the rest of the year.

This incident was not without its consequences, however. Both mothers were acutely uncomfortable with the secret marriage, and worried that at some time Lois would get pregnant, the only real issue for them. Folks count, you know, and begin counting with the public announcement. They didn't want folks to get the wrong ideas. To head off this possibility, the mothers prepared and sent an announcement of the marriage, dates and all. Folks in small towns tend to remain suspicious, however, and still insist on counting. In this case, the mothers simply provided the date from which to begin counting. The announcement satisfied the mothers, and in the final analysis, the town folks really didn't care.

One additional scene we had not fully anticipated. The service pays an allowance for members with wives. These benefits are based upon providing basic information, and signing over a statement swearing to its truth. The Navy could check, and was entitled to require documentation, should any question arise. I was uncomfortable reporting a fictitious marriage date for the service, and preferred an official, recorded date for this purpose. To reveal the Colorado wedding would blow the whistle on the breach of contract. I was not interested in revealing a breach, and preferred to continue silence about the earlier, and only legal marriage. One related issue was security clearance for access to secret and top-secret documents. Revealing a breach would raise a red flag, suggesting a degree of unreliability.

The only reasonable course was to obtain another official date for the Navy, this time in Kansas. It was not easy. We went to the Probate Court in Topeka and said we were interested in a marriage license. The clerk gave us the usual forms to complete. One of the questions was "have you ever been married?" We said Yes. The next question was about the divorce. We said that we had not been divorced. The automatic response from the clerk was that we could not get married. Rather than argue with the clerk, who had little authority, we explained that we had exceptional circumstances, and asked to talk to the judge in person. We were led to his office.

We explained the Navy contract to the judge, and our need for a date for the Navy's official records. The judge listened to our plea intently. His first response was that he had never faced this kind of a request before. Then he said the second marriage would not be legally binding, in view of the earlier marriage in Colorado. He chuckled to himself, and said he had no wish to foil our plans. Then he told the clerk to issue the license, and wished us good luck. This was step one.

The next step was to get married again. We might have gone to a Justice of the Peace to avoid any trouble, but that was not our style. Don Evans, a minister from Topeka, performed the original ceremony in Colorado. He was a friend of the family on vacation in Colorado at the time. He was fully informed of our circumstances, and had been sworn to secrecy. We called him on the phone, and asked him to assist us again. We said we were not interested in a real wedding, but would appreciate a document signing ceremony. He set up an appointment for the following Saturday morning in his office. He said he had never before had such a request.

We arrived promptly. Don pronounced us already married, and signed the papers. We needed two witnesses, so we used the church secretary and the janitor, the only other people in the church. The papers were completed in his office and filed with the State of Kansas. The following day, Don announced from the pulpit that he had married us the day before. Then he added it was the only time he ever married the same couple twice. With that public announcement, he went on to other matters. Dozens asked us after church to fill in the missing details.

With this convoluted sequence of events, I have often introduced Lois as my wife, – – by my second marriage. Some of the responses are priceless. As usual, the Navy never knew the difference.

MIRACLE AT KANSAS UNIVERSITY

My grandpa was a Baptist preacher. He did a lot of good work in his day. He also participated in a lot of rituals. They were mostly church rituals, which he used only in church. One special ritual was the dunking pool. He didn't use it very often, but when he did, it was a spectacle. A line of persons, each in a dunking robe, would enter the pool one at a time. Grandpa waded into the water first. Then he dunked each person in line down under the surface, then back up again, dripping wet. After the last person was dunked, the congregation's attention was diverted while grandpa retired to a back room to change into some dry clothes. After a ritual has been perfected, enough rubs off in one application that you never need to do it again.

The Navy had its own collection of rituals, which they instituted just as religiously. One of their favorite rituals they called drill, as in marching. Unlike grandpa, the Navy just never seemed to get it right the first time, finding it necessary to repeat the ritual over and over. Had grandpa dunked the same people over and over, they would all have become Methodists, or Presbyterians, or Seventh Day Adventists.

As for the Navy, there were several kinds of drills, all of which needed to be repeated many times. There were close-order drills, and rifle drills, and marching drills, and parade drills. Unlike my grandpa, who spoke in plain English, the drill leader always managed, indeed preferred, to garble his words so those he was drilling would have to guess what he said. In-stead of "One, two, three, four", the drill leader shouted "Houmph, houmph, hareemph, hoourh". An entire cult grew up around how each drill leader could shout his commands, yet maintain his own personal style of shouting. The cadence, timing, and voice inflections were also of great importance. If one could sing his shouting, so much the better. Unlike my grandpa, drill leaders never shouted their commands in plain English. I preferred my grandpa's style of ritual. There was something final about a simple dunking. You knew when it was over.

There was never anything final about drill in the Navy. For some obscure reason, the belief was that drill was essential for one hour every week through four years of college. Laid end to end, that was a total of 120 hours of drill, not counting travel time, the equivalent of fifteen quarter hours of coursework, or one twelfth of a complete bachelor's degree. Drill was the only event which required wearing the uniform. We learned to keep our uniforms clean and pressed for inspection. There is nothing quite as disgusting as a serviceman in a dirty uniform. The first year of drill really served a useful function by identifying the slobs early-on. It also established an awareness of our presence on campus. Beyond that, little else of value was ever accomplished.

As usual, the Navy did not share this sentiment. For three years in college, I dressed in full uniform, pressed, clean, and appropriately fit. I showed up every Thursday at noon for one hour of drill, every week, 28 weeks in a row, every year for three years. My grandpa believed that one dunking for one person was enough for a lifetime. Like my grandpa, I believed that one good dunking in drill should be enough. Then by the Grace of God, an absolute miracle occurred on the University of Kansas campus, and I was its sole benefactor. It happened this way:

All my regular classes were scheduled on Monday, Wednesday, and Friday. As fate would have it, Navy drill was the only class I had on Thursday. For me, this was acutely painful, as I had to dress in full uniform and drive to and from Lawrence, a 50-mile commute, for one hour of wasted time. During the first drill assembly in the fall of 1953, I was shocked that my name was not called from the muster list. Initially I was peeved at being overlooked. Possibly the person taking muster had simply skipped over my name on the list. An astigmatism might have impaired his vision, or maybe the noon sun was reflecting off his roster. I continued through drill to the end of class.

On the way home I reflected upon this event, and considered what responsibility I might have under this circumstance. I could advise the office secretary that my name was missing from the drill roster. She would look at the list, see that my name was missing, and assure me that the next time roll was called up yonder, my name would be there. As I was considering the Navy's habitual ritual, what made sense was to do nothing rash. I avoided the office like a plague, fearing that I might be recognized.

I did nothing rash, and pondered the possibilities throughout the week. I dressed for the second week of drill the following Thursday. I had no idea what to expect, but was quite certain that my name would be called the second time around, a simple oversight. When roll-call was taken, my name was missing again. It made little sense to continue going to drill when they didn't even know I was there. I was not inclined to go to the unit secretary to correct the oversight, the thoroughly honorable thing to do. Concerning drill, I was sadly lacking in honor. To the contrary, I was elated.

While it was somewhat risky to quit going to drill, I knew of no rule requiring me to volunteer that I had been overlooked on the drill roster. At the same time, I had real trouble going to drill for the rest of the semester. Each semester required dressing 14 times, driving 700 miles to and from Lawrence, and wasting about three hours each day in the process, when my name was not even on the drill list.

I was rapidly losing all interest in drill. If an announcement was of vital interest, I commuted to Lawrence every day with another Navy student. If an item of importance arose, he would tell me what was happening. Drill for the rest of the semester was history. I did not attend any more drills, and thoroughly enjoyed the added day of freedom each Thursday.

When the second semester rolled around, I was itching and anxious to see if it would be a repeat of the first. As necessary, I attended the first drill to confirm that my name had not been inserted covertly into the muster list. This time it was embarrassing going to drill at all, as all the other students had been assigned to permanent drill platoons, like A, B, and C. I did not have such an assignment, and had to hide in the ranks until the assembly was over, fearing that I might be recognized as belonging somewhere else.

I was all ears as they called the roll. They used the identical roster the second semester. My name wasn't called, and it appeared to be quite safe never to return to drill again. My hiding was eminently successful. When drill was over, I slithered off the field to be sure I was not recognized. Did I ever return? No! I never returned.

In my good book, three days of drill my senior year was more than adequate, a number amazingly similar to my grandpa's rule of one good dunking per person. It took the Navy three years to get it just right for me. Unlike the Navy, grandpa did it just right the first time.

DEALING WITH DOCTORS

My senior year at Kansas University was over in a flash. As a married student commuting from Topeka to Lawrence every day, there was not much to do but drive to Lawrence, go to class, study a little between classes, drive home, study a little more and go to bed. The only unusual event which made the year noteworthy was being called into the COs office. Initially I worried that the drill instructor had added my name to the class roll, and discovered that I was absent all year. On arrival I was relieved when told that I needed a pre-commissioning physical. I suspected this was unusual, as none of the other students were involved. I made an appointment to visit the Navy's regional offices in Kansas City the following Saturday.

Through the previous four years, I had completed an annual physical report. It was a comprehensive review of everything which might be of interest to the Navy. The only item of consequence was two broken bones on the left side of different vertebrae, secondary to a football injury my senior year in High School. These fractures were reported initially, and had been repeated each year three times on the annual review. As I had done everything I was expected to do, I was not concerned about my complicity in the process.

On arriving in Kansas City I met with an orthopedic surgeon. We discussed the injury in some detail, and the absence of symptoms since the cast was removed four years earlier. Then he said that a fractured vertebra was a disqualifying defect for entry into the Navy. Two fractured vertebrae were doubly disqualifying. He proceeded to show me the listings for my benefit. He was right, of course. At this point I was both concerned and upset, as I had reported the injury initially, and each subsequent year for three years. This was the fourth year. It was clear to me that the annual medical reports were not read with any deliberation at all. Or it may be that those reading the reports were not aware of the list of specific disorders, which are, in and of themselves, disqualifying. In other words, if you had the condition, you were out. I could see my Navy career, for which I had worked hard for four years, flying out the window. I could not dispute the findings I had reported, and the physician was unable to waive the listings. At that point, he might have sent me packing, – but he didn't.

He asked about documentation. When I said the only documentation would need to be obtained from the chiropractor in Clay Center, he may have had his suspicions raised. He suggested we get a fresh set of x-rays of the area. After taking new pictures, and waiting half an hour, he came in with the films. He clipped the pictures on his illuminated display and examined them carefully. He said, "Now these two fractures were in the transverse process on the left side, right". "Right, third and fourth lumbar vertebrae" I said. With this bit of confusing communication, he may well have looked at the pictures of the wrong bones. After a few more minutes, he said "I can't see any evidence of an old fracture of your vertebrae at any level, in the transverse process or in the main body of a vertebrae."

I said, "Where do we go from here?" Then he made a startling admission. It was up to him to make a determination about whether or not I had a disqualifying defect. In my ignorance, I had reported a disqualifying defect four times, initially, and on each of my annual reports. At the same time, there was no documentation that the injury actually had occurred. As his x-rays could not establish a prior history, he was really in a fix. He said that under these circumstances, he would be able to go either way. He further stated that he had no basis for deciding yea or nay in my case. Then he said "I think you really have to make this decision for me. Do you want to go into the Navy, or not?"

I waited about two seconds. I had not anticipated this option before, and had been looking forward to graduation, commissioning, and fulfilling my contract to the Navy. At that point the Navy had paid for my education through four years of college, plus many great fringe benefits. The Navy had certainly fulfilled their end of the contract, which I had signed. Now that it was time for me to fulfill my end of the contract, I had a free pass out.

"Of course, I want to go into the Navy", I said. With that response, the deed was done. He filled out the papers certifying that no evidence of the injury could be found, and sent them back through the proper channels. I drove home relieved that I did not have to struggle with another career choice just yet.

This experience introduced me to the Navy's bureaucracy of random bungling. There was no malicious intent, but it was clear that four years of medical records were never read with any understanding. Such records may have accumulated in such numbers, that nobody actually reads them, but simply filed them away for a rainy day. The rainy day had now come and gone, revealing the first of a number of bureaucratic bungles. The second set of bureaucratic bungles was not far away.

From that moment forward, I stopped reporting the old football injury in subsequent medical reports. I might have opted out, but I was within a month of graduation and commissioning. The draft was still an ugly reality. Without an x-ray showing the fracture, the Army could draft me in a minute. I had no interest in living in the trenches in the mountains of North Korea with a rifle.

As for disqualifying defects, I was trained four years, commissioned into the regular navy, ordered to active duty, and served three years sea duty in the Western Pacific with two such defects. I never gave it a second thought, and the Navy never knew the difference.

READY FOR SEA

The summer of 1954 got off to a spectacular start. The seniors at the University of Kansas walked down Mount Oread to the football stadium for their graduation ceremony. Commissioning in the regular Navy followed later the same day. The Navy had issued orders to active duty following graduation and commissioning as follows:

Upon acceptance of appointment as Ensign, Supply Corps, U. S. Navy, and when directed by the Professor of Naval Science, NROTC Unit, you will proceed to Athens, Ga., and report to the Commanding Officer, Navy Supply Corps School for temporary duty under instruction, pending further assignment to duty by the Bureau of Naval Personnel.

Our training for the Supply Corps was to receive the finishing touches in Athens, covering all aspects of supply management in the Navy. It was compressed into a twelve-week period. The school's main entrance and Winnie-Davis Hall, which housed the school's administrative offices, is shown below as it appeared in 1954.

For decades the school had been located in Bayonne, New Jersey, and had only recently been moved to Athens. Our class was the first to start training in Athens. The campus was located on the grounds of the old Normal School, and consisted of a large cluster of mostly older buildings. One building had been converted into an officers' mess, but few of the nicer amenities were otherwise available on the campus. The fresh influx of married students made it somewhat difficult to obtain adequate housing in the community, particularly since we would be short-term, 90-day residents.

We settled into a one-bedroom apartment within two blocks of the University of Georgia campus. We were within easy walking distance of Stegman Hall, where Navy students and dependents had swimming privileges. Stegman had been used during WWII and afterward as an activity center for pre-flight training of pilots. Directly across the street from Stegman was Legion Pool, where dependents could catch some rays during the hot summer days. As very few of the apartments had air conditioning, the pools were popular gathering sites.

Immediately behind our apartment was a forest of tropical undergrowth. Coming from the high plains, we were unfamiliar with the southern climate, which offered lush undergrowth and crawling vermin in abundance. We had no particular problem with the crawlers, so long as they remained outside where they belonged. One evening we allowed a dish of butter to remain in the middle of the table over-night. The next morning the butter dish was black with ants. They had beaten a path through the back door, across the kitchen, into the living room, up the table legs, and across the table to the butter dish in a single evening. Then they had accumulated in sufficient numbers to completely cover the butter until it was black with ants eating their fill. This incident set the stage for the next ninety days in which we were battling for dominion of our own apartment.

From that moment on, we scoured the stores for any appropriate weapons, which might give us an advantage against the crawlers. One early favorite was lighter fluid. It could be administered in several ways. The fluid itself was lethal when sprayed directly on the ants, but was an inefficient waste of fluid. A more dramatic effect was to pool fluid around one of their hills. A match would ignite the fluid and cripple hundreds, even thousands in a few seconds of flames. For the next hour their friends and neighbors were busy carrying off the bodies, and were momentarily distracted from entering our apartment. After a short period of trauma, they were back.

None of the commercially available sprays or chemicals were effective against ants, leaving us to our own resources. The most useful weapon we discovered was hot bacon grease. We never understood the mechanism for its effectiveness. A little hot grease on an anthill, and they abandoned ship. The grease may have sealed their underground passageways, making their homes uninhabitable. It seemed only fair. As a food source, the grease may even have clogged their little arteries, producing massive heart attacks. Whatever the mechanism, the grease was as effective as any we could find. We greased them in the mornings, and torched them in the evenings. As television was still not a useful commodity, the millions of ants provided hours of consuming entertainment throughout the day.

Except for fighting crawling insects, and the southern heat without air conditioning, school passed quickly.

Training in Athens was temporary duty, subject to re-assignment. Several days before graduation we received orders to our first permanent duty assignments. In my case they read as follows:

Upon completion of your course of instruction and when directed by your commanding officer you will regard yourself detached from temporary duty under instruction at the Navy Supply Corps School, Athens, Ga. and from such other duty as may have been assigned you; will proceed to San Francisco, Calif. and report to the Commandant, Twelfth Naval District for the first available transportation to the port in which the USS Gardiners Bay (AVP-39) may be, and upon arrival report to the commanding officer of that vessel for duty as assistant to the supply officer as the relief of Ensign David J. Griffiths, (SC), USNR, 571713/3105.

These orders set into motion the routine processing required for overseas assignments. A table of required vaccinations identified the number and kinds of shots and boosters for each destination. Going to the fleet in the Western Pacific specified a series of nine shots, seven initially, and two boosters at some subsequent time. For the next several days, the medical unit gave thousands of shots to their graduating officers, who were leaving for destinations all over the world. I received my seven shots, four in one arm and three in the other.

On reading these orders, I was reminded of the recruiting posters in windows and on street corners at the time. _Join the Navy, and See The World_, they proclaimed. As the Gardiners Bay was half way around the world from Athens, it was clear I would see the first half on my first tour of duty. I was fully vaccinated for everything except ants, and was eager to get the show on the road. The next six weeks would be an initiation into a service for which I was scarcely prepared. While the Supply Corps' motto was Ready for Sea, I was not sure I was ready, but I knew I was going.

MOTHER OF ALL JOURNEYS

The trip planned from Athens, Georgia to the Gardiner's Bay somewhere in the Western Pacific was half-way around the world. While I had traveled considerably growing up, I was completely unprepared for the events about to unfold around me. We left Athens with our few belongings and headed across the country in the middle of September. For me, the trip to the ship would take a full six weeks. The first half was uneventful, as that was the portion of the trip under my personal control. After that I gave control to the Navy for getting me the rest of the way. It was a harrowing and thoroughly unforgettable experience. As a Navy doctor had told me earlier, forget everything you have seen here today. The trip was beyond forgetting.

There were four distinct legs to the remaining part of the Journey. I arrived in San Francisco a day earlier than specified in the orders. The Twelfth Naval District was the administrative clearinghouse for all personnel going overseas, and they were to arrange for air transportation to the Gardiners Bay. At the time the military was the premiere overseas flight service. Moffett field was the Navy's base for overseas travel, and was only a few miles south of San Francisco. They made a special note of my transportation need, and in the process checked my personal records, which I was hand carrying. I was advised that travel to the Western Pacific required a series of nine shots or vaccinations, seven initially, and two more as booster shots at a subsequent time.

I was flabbergasted. First, I told them I had just received seven inoculations in the medical unit at the Navy Supply Corps School, and asked them to double-check the records for evidence of the shots. I was assured there was no record of any inoculations. In a final effort to convince the staff of my fresh shots, I lifted both sleeves to display the scars and holes. It was a futile effort, as the only compelling evidence was the recorded word in my official personnel record. They suggested I report to their medical offices for the appropriate immunizations.

The routine was familiar to me by this time, so I took an additional four shots in the left arm and three more in the right. I inquired if it would be necessary to have a double series of booster shots as well. The automatic response was no, unless they failed to record these seven shots. In that case, I would need this second set of seven shots a third time. I left the Twelfth District Headquarters feeling like a pincushion, but believed myself to be immunized against any bug, which might occur naturally in the orient. As usual, I was wrong again. I was learning the Navy way of doing things. It was not a pretty picture, yet it was precisely the same picture I would see on a recurring basis.

We had several days to rent an apartment, unload our possessions, acquire a few necessities, and prepare mentally for being separated for a few months. While I knew where I was headed, I had no information about the ship's itinerary, how long it would remain in the Orient, and when it might return. All I knew was that the ship's homeport was Alameda. The only facility in Alameda was a Naval Air Station. It was on the bay, however, and had a docking area where ships could tie up. This made some sense, as the ship was a seaplane tender, a small one. Presumably, we were capable of tending some of the needs of seaplanes, a floating service station.

On October 15 I was told to report to Moffett Field well before 0600 the following morning. I packed my bags and was dropped off at the NAS. While my orders stated first available air transportation, available means the same as space available. There was actually space available on the plane. The only things not available on the plane were the seats. The plane was a Marine R5D, the same as a Douglas DC-6B, a four-engine propeller-driven plane commonly seen at the time. A somewhat more immediate concern was the seating accommodations. The plane was not a passenger transport. It was a cargo plane which, incidentally, had jump seats along the sides. The interior of the plane was a cargo space, and was heavily packed with cargo from front to rear.

A jump seat is not really a seat. It had a canvas cot-like bottom, which ran along each side of the plane. The front edge of the seat was a metal rail to which the forward edge of the canvas was attached. Along the bulkhead was a canvas back support, which fit like a hammock. It was perfectly vertical, allowing no adjustment for reclining, or sleeping. Finally there was an additional rod five feet above the floor, which ran the length of the plane on either side. It was fitted with wrist straps, similar to those on subways in New York City for the riders who could find no place to sit. With these conveniences we settled into our jump seats for the first leg of our journey to Hawaii. This particular plane, as viewed from one of the windows, shows the right wing and engines from 8,000 feet, working just like they are supposed to work. I made a special note of the amount of grease, which had accumulated on the plane's surfaces, an issue of some concern to me.

Right two engines on Navy R5D 1954

We left Moffett and headed over the Pacific for our first stop at Barbers Point, a Naval Air Station around the bay to the west of Honolulu. This first leg was expected to take about 12 hours. Given the amenities aboard the plane, those twelve hours stretched into an eternity. We had taken off from Moffett about 0600 in the morning, and were scheduled to arrive in Hawaii by mid-afternoon, their time. Around 1030 a marine crewmember contacted each of the passengers, and asked if we were ready for our sack lunch. I said it was early, and would rather wait a while to eat.

I waited another hour or so, then contacted the marine again. He was gone for some substantial period of time before he returned with his message. He said I am terribly sorry, sir, there are no more sack lunches. I asked him to double-check his supply, as I had only asked to delay my meal, not have it consumed by others during the wait. He returned a second time with the same message. The flight continued hour after hour on an empty stomach. At 8,000 feet over the Pacific, when you are out of sack lunches, you are out of sack lunches. I asked on arrival at Barbers Point where I might find some food. I was told to check the commissary. After a twenty-minute walk, I discovered it had been secured for the balance of the afternoon. The next reasonable response I received was to take the Navy bus into Honolulu, where I could get anything I might want. I had no doubt that this was true. Given my current run of luck, I was afraid to anticipate what all I might get.

After a long wait, I boarded a Navy bus bound for Waikiki Beach, where I got off at the Royal Hawaiian. I found a local restaurant, ordered some food, and had my first meal in 28 hours. I was famished. After eating, I kicked around on the beach, wandered into a number of shops, and relaxed from the ordeal of the day. At 2200 the base bus made its routine stop in front of the

Royal Hawaiian. I boarded and took a seat near the driver along with a few other passengers. The trip from Waikiki back to Barbers Point would take about an hour. I settled into a real seat, grateful to have a padded seat and backrest, a level of comfort far surpassing the Marine's greasy airplane.

No more than five minutes into the trip, I began to experience stomach cramps. I was not exactly sure what was going on, but the early signs were not encouraging. Five more minutes into the trip I was in the midst of recurrent cramps, acute diarrhea, and bordered on losing control of my anal sphincter. I discovered the bus, while perfectly comfortable going into town, rode like a tank on the return trip. As with all navy busses, it had no restroom facilities, and I was too embarrassed to ask the driver to find a public restroom and stop. The jouncing was aggravating, and I seemed to have few alternatives to my current situation.

Then I discovered there were only two of us on the bus, the driver and me. To control the bouncing, I moved to the rear seat of the bus, stood up on the cushioned seat, then I crouched down into a squatting position. The driver may have believed I was either drunk, or out of control. Through knee action, I was able to eliminate almost all of the jouncing of the bus, and managed to survive the next half-hour ride without soiling myself or the bus. The nearest facility at Barbers Point was not nearly close enough to the last bus stop, but I managed to arrive in the nick of time. One thorough evacuation eliminated the entire problem. What little nourishment I received was sufficient to last till the next morning. A real bed that evening was a king's luxury. Early the next morning we were scheduled to resume our trip to the exotic Far East. I was rapidly losing confidence in the entire process.

Shortly after breakfast our crew and passengers boarded the same plane. We were scheduled to fly a circuitous freight route to Kwajalein Atoll, where we would drop off a load of cargo.

Several hours into the flight, we were offered the usual sack lunches. As a fast learner, I grabbed mine instantly, as I had already experienced the alternative. Throughout the flight, I noticed fresh oil streaming from the far-right engine, running along the surface, and dripping off the trailing edge of the wing. Several more hours into the flight we experienced a severe vibration, which shook the entire plane. There were no speakers on the plane, so we were left to draw our own conclusions about what was happening. Looking out the right side, it was clear the outboard engine had been feathered, and had slowed to a dead stop. Not only had the greasy plane lost power in its right engine, but headwinds were also impairing our ground speed. At the time we were halfway between Johnson Island and Kwajalein. The headwind was the deciding factor, so it was prudent to turn around and head for Johnson. We were two hours from Johnson, and with only three engines, we were considered an emergency. The picture below shows the right wing of the plane with the feathered propeller at about 8,000 feet. It was a great picture, but not a comforting experience.

Right outboard engine at 8,000 feet

To allay our fears, the captain invited each of the passengers up to the cockpit for a look around, and discuss our circumstances. To that moment, I had been fighting cigarette addiction, and had stopped smoking for almost six months. The terror at the time broke the ice, and I bummed my first cigarette shortly after we turned around. I had seen too many movies where the person about to be hanged was asked if he had a dying request. The response was almost always for a cigarette. I might have asked for a female, but there were none on the plane. I smoked cigarettes for the next ten years following that incident.

When it came my turn to go to the cockpit, I sat on a third seat between the pilot and copilot. I asked about the fluid streaming from the engines. The pilot's immediate response was that these planes seep oil constantly. If they don't drip oil, something is wrong. Then I asked about his experience with situations like this. His reply was both clear and convincing. His exact words, which I etched into memory were: "Son, during the war, I flew a plane exactly like this one with one engine gone, and a second engine on fire. We made it back with no problem." With that response, I was satisfied that we were all in good hands.

After an hour, we were joined by a military transport. Strapped to its belly was a huge lifeboat, which could be released at will, splash into the water, and presumably be available for survivors. Comforting as this thought might be, the process by which we physically transfer our bodies from a plane at 8,000 feet to a boat hanging from the belly of another plane at 8,000 feet was anything but comforting. A short time later, a third plane joined our small flock of military aircraft. It was a seaplane capable of landing to retrieve our bodies, should they survive. I concluded it was better not to anticipate the process.

We landed on Johnson Island, a beautiful atoll, which is exactly one mile long, a quarter of a mile wide, and twelve feet above sea level at its highest point. Its function was to support the airstrip, which covered the island from one end to the other. The Navy maintained the base as a support and repair facility as needed for planes straying into that part of the Pacific. We had no idea how long we might be stranded on the island. Shortly after our arrival, we were told the plane would require a replacement engine. It would have to come from Hawaii or the mainland. With this information, we prepared for an extended stay.

There were almost no trees on the island, making it difficult to imagine we had been stranded on a tropical paradise under waving palm trees. At the same time, the weather was ideal, with temperatures ranging from 78 to 82 degrees in a gentle breeze always blowing across the island. In addition to the regular meals through the commissary, and nice quarters for all on the plane, there was an officer's club, which opened every day at noon. As we were in a tropical climate, there were no windows in the club, only shutters to deflect the afternoon rains, when they came. The comfortable furniture and the cold beer turned this austere atoll into a week of R&R from the traumatic first half of the flight overseas. With luck, we might face the rest of the trip with a higher level of confidence. Seven days later the plane's engine was replaced, and was sitting on the tarmac at Johnson Island ready to go. It is shown below in October 1954, a beautiful plane from a distance. It was time to leave our tropical paradise.

R5D repaired and ready to go

Only one additional experience added to the level of anxiety I developed during the trip. We landed on Iwo Jima where we picked up a radial engine for another aircraft. It was huge, and was lashed tightly into the area directly between the wings, because its weight was a substantial load factor. We required the entire length of the runway before lifting off. When we did, the wings tips of the plane appeared to bend ten feet above their normal position. I was convinced we would hit some heavy weather, and finish plunging between them. It never happened.

Five days and two additional flights later I arrived in Sasebo where the Gardiner's Bay was scheduled to dock. I discovered deep breathing again, having survived my fourth airplane emergency. This first flight overseas was, in my experience, the *Mother of All Journeys*. Looking back upon it is a vastly superior experience.

GARDINERS BAY (AVP-39)

Following the *Mother of All Journeys*, I was greatly relieved to arrive in Sasebo in one piece. The trip from California to Sasebo by plane consumed well over three weeks. The Gardiners Bay was still operating somewhere, and had not yet arrived in port. I checked into the Bachelor Officers Quarters, and waited for the ship. It was a fascinating experience to be in Japan, an exotic eastern culture, with nothing to do but wait. After two days the ship tied-up along a dock, directly across the bay from Jane Russell mountain, a stimulating sight. Among the ships in the Navy at the time, the Gardiners Bay was equally attractive. Unlike most war ships, which bristled with guns and catapults and rockets, it looked more like the cruise ships of the day. It was painted the standard Navy gray, but otherwise was not an ominous military signal. Our presence would not send anyone a message.

From my orders, I knew I would relieve the assistant supply officer, and perform whatever other duties might be assigned. As a tender, I inferred the ship had some supplies or stores aboard which were needed by seaplanes. Beyond the fact that it was a seaplane tender, the ship's mission was almost a mystery. We actually tended seaplanes twice in 14 months. In the final analysis, the ship was a floating filling station, and provided a critical support function in earlier years. As I had discovered, airplanes were ponderously slow covering long distances, and frequently required support along the way. As new and improved airplanes came along, the need for tending seaplanes was quickly vanishing. While the ship retained little utility as a tender, it was still the prettiest little ship in the Navy. It is shown below tied alongside the pier in Alameda in December of 1954.

While the mission of the ship was not so viable, its culture was clear. There were two distinct groups of officers aboard. They were the fliers, affectionately called air-dales, and the non-fliers. Of the 16 officers on the ship, they were evenly divided between the two groups. The fliers were mostly senior grade officers. Captain Asman was their leader and the Commanding Officer of the ship, who we rarely saw. He seemed to hide in his own private quarters, and was rarely seen anywhere on the ship except the bridge. He took his meals in his own cabin, never eating with the rest of the officers in the wardroom. It must have been a lonely life. In the wardroom there were two tables of officers. The senior officers by rank sat at one table. They were exclusively the fliers, so we referred to them as the table that flew. The rest of us sat at the non-flying table. Table conversation was similarly divided, with the air-dales spending large blocks of time talking about flying and waving their hands in the air, while the rest of us discussed more earthly matters. They were all officers and gentlemen, and a thoroughly congenial group.

The executive officer deserves special mention. He occupied modest quarters immediately forward of the wardroom, but he also chose to eat by himself. In spite of his position of authority, he came across as one who was unable to make a decision. Exactly how he might function as an airplane pilot was a matter of some speculation. As executive officer of the ship, the assessment of his competence was never in doubt. When important decisions for running the ship needed to be made in a hurry, every effort was made to avoid the executive officer, who could mumble his way through every conceivable aspect of any situation. He came to be known as mumbles, for this tendency to talk aloud to himself in tones barely audible. We could never understand what he was saying, and simply accepted the mumbling as a necessary part of his work. Hopefully, he was more comfortable in an airplane.

The word at the non-flying table was that the primary mission of the ship was to provide sea duty for the fliers. It was thought that a tour of sea duty was a requisite for promotion to higher rank. If such a small ship had any more brass aboard, it would roll over. At one point we had a captain, three commanders, a lieutenant commander, and two lieutenants aboard, all fliers. The non-flying table in the wardroom included two lieutenants, four JGs, an ensign (me), and a commissioned warrant officer. Counting sleeve stripes, that is 25 stripes at the flying table on the port side of the wardroom, and only 11-plus stripes at the non-flying table on the starboard side. The chief engineer often used this imbalance to explain the ship's slight list to the port side.

A second function of the ship, because of the number of fliers aboard, was the need to be in port at least once every month. For a legitimate sailor, it really didn't matter. For a flier it was essential to make port, go to the nearest Naval Air Station, book a plane for a flight of any kind, and get into the air. This allowed them to keep their flying credentials current. One driving force behind this was the extra pay provided all pilots each and every month they flew. Over the years, their standard of living grew to require the additional flight pay for survival. Their wives and children depended upon it.

Because of the time required flying overseas, I arrived just in time to catch the ship back to the states. I did manage to relieve the officer designated in my orders before we left Sasebo. He packed his stuff and flew away, leaving me to fend for myself as the ships disbursing officer, fresh out of school. The ship had a crew of about 150 officers and men. My primary responsibility was to see they were paid every two weeks. Every payday was in cash, in amounts each individual designated, provided they had a balance in the bank. I was the bank. It was an efficient process, and throughout my tour was carried out without a major hitch. While I was the junior officer aboard, I was instantly the ships most popular officer, – because I was their paymaster. They saw me every two weeks, and went away smiling.

As the paymaster, I learned very quickly there are different kinds of money managers among the crew. Most withdrew everything they had coming in cash every two weeks. A few were so tight they squeaked, and withdrew only a pittance each payday. They scrimped and saved, and allowed a substantial balance to accumulate on the books. They were saving for a rainy day. There was also a substantial group who could hardly wait for payday. At their first opportunity with fresh cash, they would collect into small groups around the ship, and gamble until their last penny was gone. This might require several days, depending on their luck or skill at the moment, but they all knew the next payday was only a few more days away. I had been told that gambling aboard ship was strictly forbidden. To the contrary, I discovered that shooting a shipmate was strictly forbidden. Almost everything else was fine.

At the time, Korea was still a shooting war along the DMZ, and the U.S. dollar was in high demand for its black-market value. To defend against this, all the services used Military Pay Certificates (MPCs) in all combat zones of the Far East. As the ship's banker, the safe was full of two kinds of currency. It was half-full of standard greenbacks, and the other half was full of MPCs, which looked like money from a monopoly game. We were in the MPC zone when I arrived, so dealing with that was my first challenge. All ships and military bases accepted MPCs exclusively for currency. Greenbacks were not supposed to show up in the MPC zone, except in my safe.

My office aboard ship was one of the finest in the Navy. It was located on the port side of the ship, one level above the main deck, and had only outside access. I spent many hours on deck in a comfortable chair watching the sea on the ship's return trip to the states. It was so pleasant, the only work I recall was changing the MPCs back into greenbacks prior to arriving in Hawaii. With a pocket full of greenbacks, the crew was more than ready for liberty in Hawaii, prior to arrival in the continental U.S. In Pearl Harbor we tied up across from the USS Curtiss (AV-4), a large seaplane tender fit to provide all the needs required of a seaplane, plus much more. The shadow of the Gardiners Bay may be seen as a silhouette along the starboard side of this much larger ship.

After a few days in Pearl Harbor we resumed our journey to Alameda. The ride home was much rougher than expected, and demonstrated that our little cruise ship was nicely seaworthy. At one point we took green water over the bow, an experience that works best when you are secured nicely inside water-tight doors.

We tied-up in Alameda just in time to prepare for Christmas.

NATIONALIST NAVY

After relaxing a few months in Alameda, it was inevitable that we would return to the combat area in the Western Pacific. The Gardiners Bay was replenished with supplies of all kinds for its next tour of duty off the coast of China. We left for Westpac late in the spring of 1955. After a short stop in Hawaii, the balance of the crossing was uneventful. The ship had spent several years supporting patrol and air-sea rescue operations off the coast of China. As a mobile unit, it was possible to be dispatched to any part of the area on short notice. The Korean War had been in progress for several years, and was a combat zone. We were headed for the heart of the fresh conflict between the Communist Chinese and the Nationalists, headed by Chiang Kai-Shek. The site of this conflict was the Strait of Formosa. That is precisely where we were headed.

Our first stop was in Chi-lung, a port city on the northern tip of Formosa, now called Taiwan. A map and a short history lesson will make our visit come into a clear focus. Following WWII, the United Nations recognized only one China. In 1955 we were 10 years downstream from that UN agreement. Political diplomacy had been established with only one China. Military assistance was given only to one China. The United States, and all other non-Communist countries were committed to protecting one China. That one China was Nationalist China, also known as the Republic of China (ROC). When the communists consolidated power in China, they pushed the Nationalists off the mainland. Chiang moved a million of his supporters onto the islands offshore from the mainland, with the bulk moving to Taiwan. It was an island safely detached from the rest of the Asian continent by the Strait of Taiwan, a distance of about 100 miles. Chi-lung may be seen in the upper right corner of the following map. The Pescadores can be seen in the lower middle, while the Island of Quemoy is in the left-center of the map eight miles from the mainland.

From 1949, when Chiang was deposed, the Communists under Mao Tse-Tung issued regular threats that they were going to take control of Taiwan. In response, Chiang stated that the Nationalists were going to return to the mainland to resume their rightful leadership over all of China. Both sides to this conflict had been issuing these threats on a regular basis for six years to date. At the same time, the American press issued regular reports that Nationalist gunboats conducted raids on the mainland of China, shelling targets and renewing the hope that Chiang would rise again. From June 1950, the US Seventh Fleet was ordered to prevent any attacks on Taiwan, and simultaneously was blockading Taiwan from attacking the mainland. In February of 1953, the blockade portion was lifted, releasing Chiang to do his thing. From that time forward, Chiang was preparing for his return.

Much of the shooting war started during our previous tour to the area. Following removal of the Taiwan blockade, in August 1954 Chiang moved 58,000 troops from Taiwan to Quemoy, and another 15,000 to Matsu. This threatening move provoked Mao, who started an artillery bombardment of Quemoy in September. He followed this by bombing the Taschen Islands.

In November the Communist Chinese sentenced 13 US airmen shot down in the Korean War to long prison terms, causing the US to threaten the use of atomic bombs in the area. The communists also seized Jiangshan Island, 200 miles north of Taiwan, completely wiping out the Nationalist forces there. Fighting was occurring along many of the offshore islands as well as along the coast of mainland China. This was the scene we were entering in the summer of 1955.

We stopped first in Taiwan because it was the political and diplomatic nerve center for the one China policy, the home of the Nationalist Chinese. We were acknowledging their political, diplomatic, and economic position of prominence in the world. On arrival in Chi-lung, I was asked to escort the Mayor to the ship for an official visit. Little did I appreciate that he was representing three billion Chinese. All these years I thought it was because I was the lowest ranking officer in the food chain. Somehow, I missed the honor, but I did capture the 1955 event on film as shown below. From my perspective, the highlight was riding in the Captain's Gig without the Captain being present.

It's not a great picture, but I have come to appreciate exactly how many times three billion Chinese, when laid end to end, would wrap around the world. That's me below the mayor, making sure he doesn't fall back down the ladder. Following this brief official visit, the Captain chose to accompany the mayor ashore in person, relieving me of that honor.

While in Chi-lung, I was fascinated by a coal freighter, which was at anchor immediately astern. It was riding high in the water, as shown by its orange waterline. The ship was loaded almost entirely through hand labor. After three days, it was fully loaded by hundreds of Chinese laborers, and its orange waterline disappeared below the surface. Each barge is seen riding low in the water with its load of coal piled as high as possible. One man was responsible for each barge, which he moved from the back with a single oar. Moving the barges and loading the coal was a slow and arduous process, but China had not yet been mechanized, and laborers were available by the millions. It just took a little longer.

Having paid our official respects in Chi-lung, we had no need to remain in the area. From there we headed toward the Pescadores, a group of islands 25 miles west of Taiwan. The chief population center, Ma-kung, was only a short distance from an anchorage for some of the Nationalist gunboats. I eagerly anticipated seeing the gunboats that had been striking terror in the hearts of the communists on the mainland.

Throughout this tour, patrol planes were reporting all sea-based activity in the area on a continuous basis. The patrols included both land-based planes, and the more versatile PBMs, which could operate from land or protected coves as needed. Their findings were all reported through encrypted messages up and down the chain of command. We were a primary link in this communication network, which turned our crypto shack into the shipboard location that was humming continuously. All officers with secret and top-secret clearance spent many hours in the crypto shack. This required knowing how to use the latest encryption machines, including both encoding and decoding. The messages requiring distribution on the ship were circulated using covered clipboards for signatures from the appropriate personnel. While you could work yourself to death in the crypto shack, it was also one of the few places on the ship where you could lock the door and enjoy some peace and quiet.

On arriving near Ma-kung, we anchored in a protected harbor, and tendered ashore for a close-up view of the Nationalist Navy's gunboats. Two are shown below. As may be seen, they are both high and dry, suggesting that their war will be on hold at least until high tide arrives. The sailors were all collected on the boat on the right, and there were more visible on deck than could be counted. A group of officers from the Gardiners Bay is seen walking along the pier to the shore from their close-up view of these gunboats.

Chinese Nationalist gunboats

For a nation representing three billion persons, their gunboats did not inspire much confidence, but they were manned with more sailors than you could count. The boats appeared to be junks from the 19th century, which had been adapted to serve their new mission. In spite of their ancient appearance, I was told they were equipped with gray-marine diesel engines, were capable of cruising at 25 knots or better, and were highly maneuverable. Not clearly visible in the photograph were dozens of 50-caliber machine guns, which could be aimed and fired without restriction, regardless of the orientation of each boat. Their sailors should all be given ribbons for working these men-o-war in the open seas. On the Gardiners Bay, we were all awarded China Service ribbons for our operating within the war zone.

Unlike the ships of war, which were riding high and dry, the Nationalists had a supply ship that accompanied them on their missions. It was heavily endowed, and required adequate buoyancy to maintain its structural integrity. It is shown at anchor on the other side of the same pier. As may be seen, it is equally impressive, and displays a decor that complements that of the gunboats.

Nationalist Navy supply ship

Based upon appearance alone, it seemed the Nationalists could use all the protection we could provide. Without our protection, Taiwan might have become part of Communist China. As it is, Taiwan is now one of the world's most productive and modern economies. They have clearly come a long way since 1955.

In August, the Communist Chinese announced they were releasing the 13 pilots, who they had sentenced earlier to long jail terms. Accepting this as a sign of friendlier times in the Taiwan

Strait, our command chose to send us to Hong Kong for administrative and other duties as may be assigned. We left the Pescadores immediately, and headed for the British Crown Colony, leaving the Nationalist Navy to fend for itself.

STATION SHIP
HONG KONG

We made the short journey from the Taiwan Strait to Hong Kong with a high sense of anticipation. By the accounts of many sailors at the time, Hong Kong was considered the absolute title-holder as best liberty port in the world. This high title is reminiscent of the story of the old sailor, who had tested liberty ports throughout the world. As he was walking through a red-light district, one of the honeys leaned out of an upstairs window. She shouted down "Come up here, sailor, and I will give you something you have never had before". To this the old salt replied, "What do you have, Leprosy?" It was clear that a serious test of Hong Kong, as a liberty port, was about to get underway. As the Station Ship in Hong Kong, we were to play a central role in that testing process.

The following map shows the area in which we would become semi-permanent residents. The city often called Hong Kong is officially Victoria, an obvious reference to Queen Victoria and the British who controlled the area for 100 years until 1997. Because of the British influence, English was spoken by a large number of locals. The city of Victoria is located on the north side of the Island of Hong Kong, which is separated from the mainland by Victoria Harbor, a distance of several hundred yards. The area of the mainland entitled Hong Kong on the map was called the New Territories. As the British Crown Colony, the area was a hub for trade and tourism by people from all over the world for centuries. After WWII and the Japanese occupation,

Hong Kong became a favorite port for rest and recreation (R&R) for as many ships of the Navy as could manage the journey.

The approach to Hong Kong from the East is a scenic ride, with hills rising several hundred feet on both sides of the waterway. During the final portion of our entry into Victoria Harbor, we were accompanied by a group of British patrol boats, which were officially acknowledging our arrival. The escort is shown below, looking toward the mainland of China. The mountains in the distant background were beyond the New Territory, and were strictly off limits for US servicemen.

A Navy Admiral was permanently stationed in Hong Kong, and the Station Ship was under his command authority. We were scheduled to remain in Hong Kong to the end of our current tour, about December of 1955. As the Station Ship, we boarded every US Navy ship that arrived in Hong Kong, a floating tourist information center. We gave them maps that showed the off-limits areas to military personnel, distributed information about how to contact and deal with local authorities, told them to stay out of the opium dens, and provided information for use of their shore patrol. On a limited basis, we issued general supplies for those ships with critical shortages. For the smaller ships that did not have supply officers, we also held payday so the sailors would have adequate cash for liberty. Virtually all forms of cash were accepted in Hong Kong for an exchange fee.

Every day or two, at least one ship would arrive in the harbor. They were interested in being boarded as soon as possible, so they could send their crews on liberty. Our boarding parties of four to six officers and men would provide the information needed for liberty, and respond to questions or special needs to the best of our ability. Within an hour or so, we could usually provide our orientation for liberty, and return to the Gardiners Bay.

The Station Ships duties were all in addition to our regular shipboard duties which were quite heavy at times. Navy air patrols were continuing to monitor all shipping along the coast of China and Viet Nam. The Gardiners Bay continued to work as a communications hub in this reporting network. The crypto shack was a busy place for encrypting and decrypting messages on a daily basis. Because of the workload, or the need to recuperate from liberty, the ship's crew was divided into two 24-hour duty sections. Shipboard work hours remained the same as usual, but liberty was available only on alternate, off-duty days.

A major Station Ship responsibility was organizing the shore patrol for the ships in the harbor. A number of enlisted personnel worked regular shore patrol duties. While each ship was responsible for its own shore patrol, their activities were coordinated and supervised through officers and men from the Gardiners Bay. If several ships were in port at the same time, thousands of sailors and hundreds of SPs could be ashore throughout the day and night. A good feel for one of the shore patrols duties was just received in personal correspondence from one of the senior officers aboard the Gardiners Bay at the time, Commander A.E. Mix. He describes one focus of his activities as follows:

"Johnson and Johnson is a garment firm that made suits and other clothing. They were reported to me as having bought Red China material with US money, which was against the law. I assigned two shore patrol to the door of their firm, placing their business out-of-bounds. This kept all US troops from doing business there, and the Chinese people stayed away because the firm had lost face. About a week later, Father Gilligan, whose office was next to mine, advised me that Johnson and Johnson had opened for business in the Luk Wak hotel, a large building near the pier. I was advised that the hotel had a thousand rooms with a female in every one. As the hotel had four main doors, I sent eight shore patrol to place the hotel out of bounds. Even the Mayor called to plead for removing the shore patrol, but the admiral approved of my action. The next morning, I heard Father Gilligan yelling as he approached the pier 'Commander, Commander, come see!' I walked toward the Luk Wak, and saw bolts of cloth and half made suits being thrown from a second-floor window into the street by hotel employees. Johnson and Johnson was being evicted, and was no longer in business in the hotel. I contacted the Admiral and he agreed that I should remove the shore-patrol, and let the hotel resume business."

A long list of specific kinds of merchandise was presumed to originate in communist China. The merchants in Hong Kong could purchase such items for resale, and place them on the shelves along with all their other merchandise. To import the items on this list into the US legally, a Certificate of Origin was available for the merchant to complete, specifying that the goods did not originate in communist China. One could drive a Mack truck through this process, but it helped with the politics of the situation. Hong Kong was well known for its tailors. At the time it was possible to have a fully tailored dress suit from woven English woolen fabrics for about forty dollars.

While Victoria Harbor is well protected, it is not a safe harbor for ships in a major storm. The following experience, also told by Commander Mix, deals with the character of the sailors, who were testing Hong Kong as the world's finest liberty port.

"I was Senior Shore Patrol Officer of Hong Kong and had about 150 sailors as shore patrol, because the fleet was in, including carriers and cruisers. Late one afternoon we were advised that a typhoon would hit the island. My office was on Fenwick Pier on the island. We put out a general recall of all those on liberty, but the winds hit hard about dark and we had to suspend boating. Many of the ships left port to ride out the storm at sea. About 10pm, I had 2000 sailors, all wet, broke and mostly drunk waiting at the pier. In an office next to mine was a Catholic priest, Father Gilligan, who was assigned by the church to look after the sailors. He came to me and said 'Give me four men who can write, and have them write on a piece of paper, this provides a place to sleep and breakfast, and I will sign each one. Give one to each man and tell him to go anywhere he wants to'. By early morning the streets were clear. By late morning the wind let up, the ships came back into port, and we resumed normal operation. A week later the admiral asked me to contact Father Gilligan and arrange to pay for the sailor's bills. Father Gilligan told me that every sailor had paid his bill." (Many thanks to Mixer for the above stories)

After well over two months in Hong Kong, we had settled into a comfortable routine as Station Ship. It came to an abrupt halt with urgent orders to proceed immediately to Nha Trang, Viet Nam. We were to rescue a P5M crew and patrol plane, which had lost an engine. Within hours, we recalled the troops, weighed anchor, and headed for Nha Trang.

THE PAPER TIGER

Except for one emergency trip to Viet Nam, the Gardiners Bay spent over two months as the Station Ship Hong Kong monitoring Victoria Harbor. Late in the tour, the captain's relief arrived in Hong Kong. Preparations were made for the change of command aboard ship, an event to occur on the following Saturday morning precisely at noon. At that moment, responsibility for operation of the ship passed from the old captain to the new captain, with no buck passing in between. The ship's deck log documents that moment, and the new commanding officer is in charge of everything from that point forward.

All preparations for the relieving ceremony were progressing nicely. The shipboard records and reports were all in order. Such a major event aboard ship can't be adequately celebrated without a party. Unlike the British, US Navy ships forbid the consumption of alcoholic beverages while aboard. These rules then change dramatically once the crew is ashore. In the best Navy tradition, it follows that the party would have to be held ashore. And so it was. The party plans were set for Friday evening just before the Saturday relieving ceremony. I had no idea that I was to become an integral part of the plans.

On Friday around 1700, I was advised that I should get ready to relieve the officer of the day (OD) on the quarterdeck within an hour. This was a little strange, as I was not on any roster for OD duty, and had never served in that regular capacity aboard ship before. I reviewed this circumstance carefully from my perspective, the only perspective available to me.

By rank, I was not quite as low as the commissioned warrant

officer, who had 25 years of credible Navy experience, an old salt by any measure. By contrast, I was a boot ensign, a staff supply officer of all things, and was scarcely qualified to walk the decks while underway. For the powers aboard ship to turn responsibility for the ship over to me was an incredible stretch. All I could think was its got to be one hell of a party.

Then on the other hand I saw no particular problem with it, as we were securely anchored in port. As the junior officer in the day's duty section, it made some sense. I had worked one deck watch as a midshipman on the battleship Missouri two years earlier, and I would have an experienced chief petty officer available on board. There were few actual preparations for me to make. About 1800, I relieved the OD, and logged myself in as the OD, my maiden voyage. A navy ship's deck log is a daily chronology of certain events for administrative and legal purposes, the captain's official record of what's happening aboard ship. I was not sure what events were appropriate to record, but believed that covering my own tail (CYA) might be legally appropriate under the circumstances.

Within a half hour, the officers began leaving the ship for the relieving party ashore. An hour later, the last officer who was qualified to get the ship underway walked down the gangway to the captain's gig, and was shuttled ashore. With his departure, I recorded in the deck log that the last officer qualified to get the ship underway departed from the ship. I recorded the exact time of his departure. Around 2330, about four hours later, the first officer qualified to get the ship underway returned to the ship. I duly recorded this event in the ships log with the exact time of his return. From my perspective, it was no big deal, as it was strictly a means to cover my legal tail in the event of some unexpected emergency, for which I might not be qualified by either training or experience. As soon as the earlier OD returned to the ship, he relieved me, and I hit the sack.

When Saturday morning arrived, the relieving ceremony at

noon was not far off. Around 1000 in the morning, Commander Mix pulled me aside and said something like Bob, we have a problem with the deck log. I explained that I was simply covering my legal a– for whatever contingencies might have occurred. I understood him to ask that I remove the entries from the log, and everything would be fine. I saw no problem with the entries, as they were factual, strictly accurate, and covered me legally. In all probability, he responded that the entries were simply not acceptable as they were, and suggested that we both visit the executive officer, – to mediate the dispute.

The next stop was with the executive officer in his cabin. I was not exactly sure how the Exec. would mediate, but he performed as he usually did. He considered the circumstances, examined the entries carefully, mumbled to himself an assortment of utterances, many of which were unintelligible, and in the final analysis came down squarely on both sides of the issue. Then he likely mumbled something about discussing it with the captain. As a mediator, the Executive Officer provided no resolution acceptable to Commander Mix, so we left.

It was at about this point that I had a vision of the logbook, elevated to a position of such prominence that it was no longer puzzling. It had turned into the Holy Grail, and was about to be enshrined through the ceremony, which was to follow. As the centerpiece of the relieving ceremony, it had been bronzed and wrapped in red, white, and blue ribbons. It was open to the page I had defaced with my entries, as it was handed from one captain to the next, thereby embarrassing both. Immediately thereafter, I had a second vision in which I saw my body swinging from the mainmast in full dress blue uniform, with a sign attached: No CYA on my watch. It was signed E.C. Asman, Captain, USN, Commanding Officer, Gardiners Bay (AVP-39). Suddenly it occurred to me that, in the vernacular of the sailors, I had seriously pissed-off the wrong people.

In the discussion that ensued, I was offered an option to visit with the captain, or deal with the unacceptable entries. I had no interest in seeing the captain, and stated that I would be happy to draw a line through the entries and initial the corrections in the log. This option was accepted. A single line was ruled through each of the two entries, and I initialed both. So long as they remained legible, I had no problem with this modification. To this day, I have no idea who blew the whistle on my log entries. It might have been Commander Mix, or the OD who I relieved, or the old captain who was leaving. With confidence, I can say it was certainly not the executive officer.

The relieving ceremony was held as scheduled, the new CO took charge of the Gardiners Bay, with all its many fine folks, – who had thrown one heck of a party.

Through the years to that time, I had heard many stories about the paper tiger, which puts up a mighty fight until it comes time for serious combat. This was precisely my situation. In the words of the senior officers on the Station Ship, all of whom were fliers, I caught fire, and went down in flames. To my distress on that day, I was the paper tiger.

After reading the above narrative, Commander Mix sent the following personal correspondence 22 November, 2001:

"Just read the Paper Tiger. As you knew, my motivation was to keep you in the Navy, because you were a keeper. When I was skipper of the VP-19, I got away with a similar stunt. An order came from the Navy's Bureau of Aeronautics that to get a spare part, we had to first turn the old part in. I sent my mechanics to the bone yard and "rescued" the spare parts I needed in advance, and turned them in for on hand supplies. One room was set up with parts bins all labeled. During administrative inspection, the admiral came through and knew what I had done. When one of his officers complained, he said 'Orders are for compliance by idiots, but guidance of reasonable men'. Happy Thanksgiving, Art Mix"

AVP to the rescue

We had become quite comfortable as Station Ship in Hong Kong, and like many good things, it would not last. Commander Art Mix describes the journey to Nha Trang as follows:

The Gardiners Bay received an urgent message to proceed to Nha Trang, Viet Nam to rescue a P5M crew that landed there after losing an engine. At midnight we got underway with Capt. Wally Short as the Commanding Officer and I was navigator. The only charts we had of Nha Trang were French, with English notation, published in 1906. I took a course well off shore to avoid shore obstructions and an ocean current that would have slowed us down. I planned a 90-degree right turn to head directly into Nha Trang when we reached the proper latitude. We made the turn and were due on site at daybreak. The Captain and I kept a close watch on the radar because we were worried about the accuracy of the charts. Just off the starboard bow an island appeared on the radar, but the charts showed two islands at that location. The Captain spoke over my shoulder as I was checking the radar; "How much do you bet that is the right island, he asked? I replied, "I am betting my career and yours too". Right on schedule, the island, as it appeared on the radar, split into two islands just as the chart showed, and we made anchorage with no problem. Captain Short has kidded me about this many times since.

As expected, the plane and its crew were in the harbor, anxiously awaiting our arrival. We housed the plane's crew, and prepared the plane to be picked up by a larger tender, as soon as it might arrive. The plane shown above is tethered to the fantail of the Gardiners Bay while we provide service. After doing our duty, we were under no obligation to return to Hong Kong with the same degree of urgency. Two days liberty in Nha Trang appeared to be in order. A few rare experiences were not far away.

Not far from our anchorage near Nha Trang was the above patrol craft with dozens of flags flying. More fascinating was the ingenious fishing rig shown this side of the ship. As may be seen, a net is suspended from four poles, which are apparently hinged on the bottom of the bay. As may be seen, there is also a line that runs from the net to the shore, where it is attached to the ladder, seen extending from the shore on the right. The boat under the line makes a complete fishing system, and was operated by a single native. It works this way: The fisherman moves onto the ladder, unties the line holding the net above the water, and lets the line out. He extends the line until the net, and all four poles are flat on the bottom of the bay. Then the fisherman throws all kinds of attractive, smelly, and rotten bait into the water over the net.

The fisherman then takes a short siesta while the fish gather above his net. After an abundant gathering of fish starts feeding over his net, he pulls the line very slowly back toward the shore, lifting the four poles and the net in the process. He can see immediately whether there are fish in his net. For a worthy catch, he gets into the boat, pushes himself under and into the middle of the net. There he opens the trap door in the center of the net, and the fish fall into his boat. He poles himself back to the ladder where he crawls ashore with his fish. He remains perfectly dry throughout this exercise. With the proper amount of rotten bait, he can fish to his heart's content. Then he cleans the fish and sells them in the open market. Salvaging his cleanings from the day before, he has enough rotten bait for the next day's fishing. It is almost a perpetual motion business, worthy of a fast fishing franchise.

Had the above observation been the extent of our contact with food in Nha Trang, we would all be fortunate. It was not to be.

SPUDS AND SLIT SKIRTS

The Gardiners Bay had not been able to re-supply since leaving the states several months earlier. When we arrived in Nha Trang, we had no critical shortages, but select consumables were in short supply. Fresh eggs had been gone for weeks, and all milk was reconstituted from powder. Most of the fresh vegetables were totally exhausted. At the time, vegetables grown throughout the Orient were huge, inexpensive, and very attractive to the eye. Unfortunately, most were raised in night soil, which accounts for their size and beauty. It also accounts for chronic diarrhea for those without the native's immunity. For the unwashed, night soil is regular soil when fertilized with human feces. A thorough washing is useless, as the problem is not on the surface of the vegetables. The only solution was a thorough cooking. We discovered that most sailors were not interested in cooked lettuce or cabbage. Unlike the English, hot tomatoes were not high on the sailors' edible food chain, except for the two-legged variety.

Because of the vegetable problem, the Army operated large vegetable farms throughout Japan. We had not been close to one of these sources for re-supply, and had not seen a Navy provision ship. We did have a large selection of Army training films, which were designed to encourage healthy contact with the local ladies on liberty. At the time, a rumor was circulating widely aboard ship that a few of the area's honeys had a form of social disease that had descended from alligators. It was not a visible disorder, like scales or long sharp teeth, and it required several days to culture in a tube. Most sailors were not interested in the culturing process. The ship's doctor had a large assortment of shots and remedies for many such diseases. However, the story was that he had little available to treat animal disorders, except for painkillers, and a great bedside manner for those who lined-up outside sickbay the morning after.

The above issues set the stage for liberty in Nha Trang that was about to get underway. Some of the sailors had been here before, and knew exactly where to go for a hot meal and dessert.

My time ashore was to be spent on a special assignment from the supply officer, whose provisions were depleted. It seems we had run completely out of potatoes, and the captain insisted that potatoes be purchased ashore. I had absolutely nothing to do with potatoes, but the reasoning was that I had money, which could be exchanged for anything I wanted. All sailors know this to be true. On the surface it was a simple request, and the market in Nha Trang was only a few minutes away. I was to go ashore with money, and return with a re-supply of potatoes. In view of night soil plague and the Army training films, my appetite for anything which might be purchased ashore was completely extinguished.

Officially, I was in a catch-22. I had been carefully indoctrinated about exactly whose money I was spending. It was not my money, but Uncle Sam's money. If I spend it, I better document exactly what I spend it for. If Uncle Sam later determines that I had not spent it wisely, I was personally responsible to cover what was called an exception. All exceptions I pay for from personal funds. A large number of stories, all designed to make the point, described disbursing officers spending time in Leavenworth for failure to go by the book. For this reason, I combed through five Bureau of Supplies and Accounts Manuals in order to find the proper authority for potato purchases. I could not find a single statement which said "The captain told me and I am telling you to go ashore and buy potatoes". In the courts, this is called hearsay, and is not admissible. Among sailors, it is a rumor, at best. When the captain says it aboard ship, it is law, but I still go to jail. Somehow it just didn't seem quite fair, but it did keep most of us honest.

To cover my tracks (CYA), I consulted the manual dealing with provisions, which includes potatoes. Deep in that manual, I found an obscure provision for emergency purchases that referenced a 1916 law enacted by congress. Citing this law, I filled out papers stating that "the captain declared a potato emergency", thereby authorizing me to purchase potatoes in the open market. I was willing to gamble $50 of my own money that it was not a rumor. This is called covering your a– by placing a very small bet.

It was at about this point that I had another of my visions. As I was preparing the papers, when I got to the statement saying "The captain declared a potato emergency", he appeared over my shoulder, and read the statement aloud as I wrote it. Then he said "What do you want to bet this statement is true?" I replied "I am betting my career, my whole career, and nothing but my career, so help me God, plus fifty bucks of my own". Then my vision flashed immediately to a small cell in Leavenworth. I looked around my small cell, and the captain was nowhere to be seen. I have been in hiding ever since!

Hurdle two was to get some local currency, which the natives would recognize. The disbursing manual specified that when carrying currency ashore, a sidearm and locked money box are required. So there I went with a gun and my personal wager of fifty bucks in a lockbox. We exchanged the greenbacks for local currency. I elected to spend the entire wad on emergency potatoes, having no idea how many potatoes that might produce. Then we headed for the market.

The above picture captured my first view of the open market in Nha Trang. It looked far worse than the scullery aboard ship after Thanksgiving dinner. It is also where we started our search for spuds. The streets were littered with every form of rubbish, as may be seen. I was fascinated by the triangular appearing sunshades, which were worn only by the women. In the foreground is a distinctive bicycle taxicab and driver. The taxi carried only one person, who rode in the cab facing the rear. From this point, as we moved deeper into the market, the view did not improve.

We found no one merchant who had an adequate supply of potatoes, so we purchased all that was available from each vendor we found. For collecting the spuds and carrying them back to the ship, we bought three large woven baskets for a fraction of our fifty bucks. Within fifteen or twenty minutes, we had seen most of the market, and had purchased as many potatoes as we could carry back to the jeep.

If the sailors had seen the market, they might have refused to eat the fresh spuds. Most had little interest in the market, choosing the local honeys over potatoes every time. In the above picture, the two shapely ladies on the left deserve special attention. Both are wearing a traditional garment that is split to the waist along both sides, producing a front flap and a rear flap. On cool mornings, they wear silky, black full-length pants. As the day warms, the pants come off, displaying an abundance of feminine flesh, an exotic view not seen elsewhere in my experience.

The Vietnamese women were all nicely trim, and in the long garments, on a warm day, produced great views from any angle. Most were very attractive, until they smiled. The smile broke the spell, revealing bright red-purple teeth from chewing beetle nuts. Beetle nuts are dark purple seed-like objects. I was told they are mildly narcotic, and are widely consumed by the women throughout much of Southeast Asia. Whatever kind of high they produced is unknown. The stain, however, is permanent, leaving the teeth bright red-purple for life.

When we returned to the ship, we had spent all the local currency. In exchange we had a fair pile of small potatoes, and three very fine native baskets. We did not weigh the potatoes, but they were miniscule when compared with the Idaho variety. As we had purchased them from a dozen vendors, we were certain the mixture contained an assortment of contaminants capable of flushing out the GI tract for several days running.

Most of the spuds were considered too small to peel by hand, so the cooks used the mechanical peelers. They started with small potatoes, and ended with potato nuggets. The three baskets of potatoes fed the crew only a time or two, as most of each potato went down the drain from the peeler. Fortunately, the Gardiners Bay was underway before we ran out of potatoes again, thereby avoiding the next great potato famine.

The return to our friendly anchorage in Hong Kong was a pleasant relief. Shortly thereafter, a Navy provision ship arrived in the harbor, and we restocked with an abundance of potatoes, certified to be free of bubonic plague. This process was a vast improvement over our emergency purchases in Viet Nam. By contrast, there was no way to improve upon the slit skirts, which the sailors thoroughly enjoyed every day in Nha Trang.

MARY SOO

Hong Kong has been judged the absolute best liberty port in the world. This high rating is from sailors who have tested liberty all over the world. When sailors speak of liberty ports, it is accepted that the ladies are not far away, if only for the great scenery they provide. After spending several months in Hong Kong, one lady emerges who stands head and shoulders above all the rest. She was one of a kind, and provided an incomparable service for the sailors on extended stays in the city. She is known throughout the world, and in one magazine, was the featured centerfold. She is Hong Kong's infamous Mary Soo.

Unlike other ladies, she was granted freedom to move around select ships in the harbor without restriction, plying her trade, and in the process, relieved many sailors aboard ship, whose duties were onerous. Like many ladies, she was a shrewd businessperson, and never passed up a profitable deal. And like most, she accepted no checks, no credit, and no promises. She worked strictly under contract, and required payment for services as rendered. Some claimed she was an artist, enhancing each sailor's world with her special touch. Others said she was a workhorse, dedicated to an incomparable service. On the Gardiners Bay we knew her intimately. We had an understanding with Mary Soo.

While Mary Soo worked well for her customers, she was also the head honcho lady, the madam working a bevy of like-minded and well-trained girls. They arrived at the ship each and every day on their sampans, small boats that were perfectly adapted to working at the water's edge. Most surprising was that Mary Soo and all her girls provided their services free for our garbage, no questions asked. Following the strictest of standards, the leftovers from the mess-hall after each meal were collected in individual containers and delivered to Mary Soo each day. To receive such fine service for that which otherwise would be thrown away, was an unbelievable bonus value. She is shown below with some of her girls, hovering next to the Gardiners Bay on one of her sampans.

From top to bottom, stem to stern, all around, she painted the ship. On this day, with long poles in hand, they are painting the ship's hull with loving care. We provide the paint, and they paint the ship for the garbage, no questions asked. It was a big ship, and required long poles, many girls, and many days for a single coat. Exactly how many coats of paint might have been applied is not known. It was such a fine arrangement, the ship was painted over, and over, and over until it was just right. Following is a glamour shot of the Gardiners Bay at anchor. Sun covers on the bow's main deck and 01-level are prepared for hanging out in style, while Mary Soo and her girls slave away. What a novel way to relieve the sailors.

She kept our beautiful little ship in top shape, and carried off the excess food as a bonus. It is understood that she gave much of the food to her many working girls. What they did not want, she sold on the streets throughout Hong Kong. Through this process, we were feeding those many starving Chinese we had heard so much about.

In the late fall, 1955, we came to the end of our tour as Station Ship, and knew we would miss Hong Kong. We knew that many tears would be shed. For our departure, Mary Soo planned a mighty going away celebration. She rigged a sampan with one of her many long poles, and from the high end of the pole suspended a twelve-foot long cluster of firecrackers. Then she summoned four of her most loyal girls to follow us out of the harbor. As we pulled away, she lit the firecrackers. For five minutes the crackers swished like the tail of an angry dragon, almost blowing Mary Soo and her girls out of the water in the process. Then we were gone.

As we passed out of sight, Mary Soo shed buckets of tears,

because she knew we were taking all our garbage with us. What a deal!

HAMILTON COUNTY (LST-802)

With Christmas 1955 not far away, the Gardiners Bay returned to its homeport in Alameda. My relief arrived to assume the duties as disbursing officer. He double checked the pay records, counted the money in the safe, and signed the papers lifting my primary job on the ship. I had received orders to report to the Hamilton County (LST-802) to relieve the supply officer of that ship. The ships homeport was Long Beach, and was scheduled to remain stateside for several months. I knew nothing about the ship, but had seen an LST from a distance during exercises in Little Creek three years earlier. As we would not be returning to the bay area, we packed our stuff, loaded the car, and headed east.

After a short Christmas visit in Kansas, we took the southern route back to Long Beach. The Hamilton County was in port. It was a beautiful – hulk. All the suave and debonair that accompanied the Gardiners Bay was left behind when they designed the LST. Before I could say Jack Robinson, I had moved from club level suites to steerage.

The above 1950 Navy Archive picture of the 802 was taken in Inchon, Korea. It shows the bow doors open, and its ramp on the beach for loading or unloading cargo or personnel. While the ship is over 300 feet long, the forward two-thirds is a single tank-deck, a long narrow warehouse in which may be placed anything that fits. With this huge cargo space, it was perfectly adapted for moving objects large and small and as many men, women, and children with their personal belongings as could be crammed in for a short trip. To commemorate the valuable contribution of the LST, a bronze sculpture was erected in Washington DC entitled Large Slow Target. The Hamilton County was an outstanding, but traditional ship of this class for eleven years until 1 July 1955, six months before I reported for duty. The ship's distinguished service record included one WWII battle star, and seven Korean battle stars, with service from Guadalcanal, Saipan, and Okinawa to Inchon and Pusan.

As ships go, the LST was designed for making one trip across the ocean, – slowly. They had a tendency to wallow through the waves like a surfboard. With their flat bottom, if the bow raised much above the waves, its fall to the water produced a pounding jolt initially, then a slow longitudinal gyration, which can be clearly observed from either end of the ship. This vibration may last for three or four seconds before it subsides, a beautiful imitation of Elvis the Pelvis, the heartthrob at the time. LSTs were virtually unsinkable because of the honeycomb structure over which they were built. At their top speed of 10 knots, they created a dashing and awesome spectacle, striking terror in the hearts of her enemies and her crew alike.

The 802 had performed many evacuations of civilians, military personnel and equipment through the years. As such, the tank deck became the final resting place for whatever the evacuees did not want, or could not find as they left the ship. The most recent evacuation was the previous year from the Taschen Islands to Formosa. The story was that the rubbish was several feet deep on the tank deck, and was carried off the ship by the truckload. The untold story included a ton or two of wharf rats which came aboard with the refugees, and refused to leave.

The details of the rat story tied together the evacuation of refugees to the structure of the LST, which included thousands of nooks and crannies in which rodents, mostly rats, could hide forever. Most rats, I learned, were nocturnal, preferring to come out only after dark. The nooks and crannies in the ship were dark most of the time, making it an ideal habitat for nocturnal animals. Because of the infestation, it was said that port authorities required the 802 to place its rat guards on the lines securing the ship to the dock in reverse, thus keeping the rats from going ashore. The ship was a virtual buffet of leavings and hiding places, and unlike every good sailor, there was no good reason for any rat to go ashore.

Like the unsinkable Molly Brown, the Navy discovered that the old Ts were amazingly versatile, and could be converted to dozens of specialized uses with minor modifications. With this in mind, it fell the lot of the 802 to become the newest of three minesweeper tenders. In this role, it was to be outfitted to supply many of those things needed by minesweepers for clearing waterways of explosive devices. On 1 July 1955 a magnificent transformation was begun, converting the ship into a modern and sleek man-o-war, – hulk. Her new assignment earned it the additional name, Hamilton County, to be appended to the front of its old number, USS LST-802. In the following picture, the

Hamilton County is ready for exercises off Catalina Island. Just above the yellow mines is a railing that surrounds the 01 level deck just forward of the bridge. This is the deck where Captain Quegg, on a similar ship, made many of his announcements to the crew. It was also where he maintained his pet tree, until Ensign Pulver threw it overboard.

On reporting aboard the captain was ashore, and was not expected to return till the next day. First, I found the supply officer who I was to relieve. He was called up as a reservist, and was looking forward to his return to civilian life. He took me through the ship and introduced me to the men in the Supply Division. We made a quick tour of the supply areas for which the department was responsible. That area covered about 80% of the ship below the main deck, plus the officers' quarters and wardroom facilities. Then he filled me in on the recent story of the supply department from his perspective. It was not pretty, and bore no relationship to supply management as taught in school. I was fortunate to miss the shipyard modifications and re-supply process for its new mission.

The small group of officers had all arrived within the past few months. They were young, alert, and well educated, as all had earned at least a bachelor's degree from some college or university. They were all ensigns, or newly promoted JGs, like me. The executive officer, a former merchant marine for a dozen years, was on his second Navy tour as a lieutenant JG. By contrast, the captain was reported to have completed all eight years in elementary school quite successfully. His credentials as a seaman were never in question, but he was reported to make derogatory references to those with an education, which included all of us. The communications officer, a graduate of Harvard, received an abundance of such comments, owing to his New England accent, coming from the Ivy League, and for driving a three-wheel Morgan. The stage was nicely set for a rerun of the Caine Mutiny.

With the serious problems in the Supply Department, I didn't know if I was about to take on the role of Mr. Roberts or Ensign Pulver, but I knew I was on the right ship. Having met the officers, the only thing left to do was meet Captain Quegg. I wondered if he would juggle three little steel balls in the palm of his right hand. The next day in Long Beach would tell the story.

On arriving aboard ship the next day, I went first to the captain's quarters. The captain was Lieutenant Vernon W. Weatherby, a mustang who had arisen from the ranks of submariners. I reported myself for duty.

"Great little supply ship you have here, Captain," I added.

He smiled broadly, showing his missing front teeth. Then he was speechless for several seconds. The delay suggested that he had never really thought of the ship that way before. It could be that he had a rush of a dozen derogatory comments, and he just didn't know which one to choke out first.

"Is this a supply ship?" he asked.

In that moment, I knew it was going to be a very long, action-packed tour of duty. As all sailors do, I knew I would come to love this great little ship. As I left his quarters, I could hear the sound of those three little steel balls.

"Clack, clack, clack, clack"

LOAD LIST FROM HELL

The Hamilton County was a reasonably small ship with about 100 officers and men. About a third was the Supply Department. While I was the only officer in the department, a few sailors with bachelor's degrees enlisted in the Navy to avoid the alternatives. As such they served only two-year terms. The department had several such sailors, a nice bonus for handling the departments functions. As most were bachelors, they managed to survive on Seaman Second Class pay, together with a few seasoned veterans in the department.

The Supply Department included a host of somewhat discrete supply functions, a few of them common to the larger ships in the Navy. They included the following:

1: Enlisted Mess: The ships cooks provided three squares a day for all the crew, and were particularly proud of the breakfast meal that featured SOS, a favorite of many of the sailors. In addition to food preparation and eating areas, food storage included non-perishable, dry, and refrigerated storage.

2: Wardroom and Officers' Quarters: Stewards distributed food from the enlisted mess, and took care of the officers' cabins.

3: Ship's Store: The corner convenience store sold cigarettes, candy bars, film, shaving supplies, and hundreds of other personal items.

4: Geedunk Stand: The ships soda fountain and ice cream shop.

5: Clothing and Small Stores included uniforms, shoes, and navy issue boxer shorts with ships embroidered on each pair.

6: Laundry services washed and pressed uniforms for all hands aboard.

7: General Stores included commonly required consumables like office supplies, tools, cleaning products, toilet paper, mops, and holystones. After the renovation, the ship took on additional supplies for flagship and tender operations.

8: Aviation repair parts included a separate cage of spare parts for support of a HUP-2 helicopter, which was assigned to the ship.

9: Minesweeping Gear: This included many of the things needed for use by minesweepers.

10. Disbursing was the ships banking function and payroll. Individual accounts were maintained for all hands on the ship. Payday was held in cash every two weeks. The amounts paid were as requested by each individual. Unpaid balances accrued on each pay record for future payments.

All the above functions were mine, together with the skills and training of men in the department. My preliminary assessment of the department was that everything was in fair shape, except for one very serious problem, the newly acquired minesweeping gear and supplies. All the items to be supplied were included in a load list prepared by the Commander of Mine Forces, Pacific Fleet. It was the guts for our existence as a minesweeper tender, and was the reason for the ship's conversion only six months prior to my reporting aboard. As the Hamilton County was the third LST converted to a minesweeper tender, one might think the bugs would have been worked out of the load of supplies needed to do the job. Not so.

When all the structural modifications to the ship were complete, the ship moved to a dock area adjacent to a railroad track. Then railroad flatcars and boxcars filled with items on the load list began arriving alongside the ship for loading. As each car was unloaded, new cars arrived in what appeared to be an endless stream of such cars. The following is a reconstruction of the conversations that were likely to have occurred during this loading process. The first is between the Commander of Mine Forces, Pacific Fleet and Captain Vernon Weatherby on the Hamilton County.

"Admiral, this is Captain Weatherby on the Hamilton County. We just tied up along the dock in the shipyard to receive minesweeping gear. There is a whole string of railroad flatcars and boxcars, and I understand we are supposed to load all of it aboard the ship as soon as possible. Just how many cars will we be receiving, and where are we supposed to put it all?"

"Vernon" he said "There should be a load list of the equipment you are receiving. It itemizes everything you will get in the next few days. We have been busy loading everything we could find in our warehouses that you might need. We have a lot of stuff coming from other warehouses and some is being shipped directly from manufacturers. I really have no idea how much stuff you will be receiving, but you should do your best to store it on the ship's tank deck."

"Admiral, I don't remember receiving any list. Just who is responsible for all this stuff?"

"Vernon, your supply officer should have a copy of the complete list, and should know how to take care of it. It is really his responsibility aboard your ship. You might want to talk to him about the stuff that is coming aboard."

"Thanks, Admiral", said the Captain "I'll do that right away."

Shortly after this conversation, Captain Weatherby called the supply officer, and asked him to bring the load list up to his quarters.

"Come in, George", said the captain. "I just called the Admiral at ComMinePac about the gear we are loading aboard the ship. I was concerned about how much there was, and how long it was going to take to get it all aboard. Do you have the list of gear?"

"Yes, Captain. Here it is. Its a pretty long list, and we only have one copy of it."

Have you had a chance to study it?

"No, sir. We just received the list in the mail yesterday from ComMinePac. We started loading it aboard early this morning, and I really haven't had time to study it in detail."

"Are we going to have room for it on the tank deck?" asked the Captain? "When I saw the string of railroad cars on the dock with gear for us to take aboard, I wanted to know how many railroad cars we would be receiving, and where we would put it all. The admiral said you would be responsible for it."

"Yes sir. We will be storing most of it on the tank deck. Some of the items are larger than we can physically handle aboard the ship. We can lower these large items through the hatch onto the tank deck, but we have no way to move them once they are there. I have no idea how many items of this size are on the list. It would be best for us to delay loading these items until after the smaller stuff has all come aboard. Then maybe we can decide whether to load it on the main deck, or send it back to the Admirals warehouse ashore."

"What will the Admiral think if we did that?" asked the captain.

"I really have no idea." George said. "If we take it aboard, we should keep it on the main deck so we can move it using the ship's electric booms. If we put it on the tank deck, it will block access through the hatch to everything else, and we won't be able to move around on the tank deck at all."

"I really have mixed feelings about storing a bunch of supplies on the main deck said the captain, particularly when I have no idea how many items there will be, and how much they weigh. We can't have very much because the helicopter requires a margin for clearance of its rotors. There is also a problem with the ships stability."

"If you like, Captain, I will go through the load list to see how many items are so large we will have a problem handling them on the tank deck. We can just leave them ashore, if you prefer."

"Why don't you do that, George, and get back to me if you think there might be a problem with it."

"Aye, Aye, Captain. By your leave, sir."

Over the next few days, as much stuff as could be crammed onto the tank deck arrived and was accounted for on the load list by a single check-mark. At this point, the supply officer called on the captain again.

"Captain, we have stacked as much mine-sweeping gear on the tank deck as we can handle. The pile is from ten to fifteen feet high in some places, and we are beginning to have trouble getting the forklifts through the center passageway. I think we have a record of everything we have taken aboard, but I would suggest that we stop loading any more stuff."

"How much is still ashore?" asked the captain.

"There are dozens of individual items we left ashore because they were just too big for us to handle aboard the ship, and there are a number of boxcars and flatcars still on the tracks waiting to be unloaded that we haven't touched. I have no idea how many cars have not yet arrived, but some additional railroad cars just arrived today."

"We are taking an additional foot of draft from what we have loaded. I am not sure I want any more stuff on board either." said the captain. "I will call the admiral and tell him we have taken as much on board as the ship can handle, and will be sending everything that is left back to him."

"When you talk to the admiral, tell him that we unloaded the railroad cars on a first come, first served basis, as the cars did not arrive according to any priority system that we know about," said George. "You better tell him that there are a number of railroad cars in the loading area that we couldn't get to at all. In addition, there are several dozen items that were too large for us to put aboard the ship at all, and we left those items on the dock area by the railroad."

Shortly thereafter the captain called the Admiral.

"Admiral, this is Captain Weatherby on the Hamilton County. I just talked to the supply officer about the minesweeping gear we have been loading. He said we have loaded all we can handle aboard the ship. A number of items were just too big for us to get on the ship at all. We left them on the dock near the railroad tracks. There are also a number of railroad cars of gear that we didn't even get to.

Vernon, said the admiral, did you get the important stuff aboard?

"The supply officer said we took the cars on a first come, first served basis. If the most important stuff was in the first cars we unloaded, then we got some of the most important stuff. Some of the items were too big for us to handle aboard the ship at all, and that gear we left ashore."

"Why didn't you put the big stuff on the main deck?" asked

the admiral.

"Because the helicopter requires clearance for its rotor blades. Stability is also a problem, as we are taking an additional foot of draft without putting anything on the main deck. We couldn't have gear stacked above the main deck. said the captain.

"Just what am I supposed to do with all the gear you are returning?" asked the admiral.

"Maybe you can find the people who made up that list of gear, and see if they can put it where the sun doesn't shine," replied the captain.

And so it was. The tank deck was loaded with minesweeping gear for several days. The orientation at the time was to get as much of the gear aboard as possible. As soon as the maximum was reached, the loading was terminated, and all additional gear was returned to the sender.

On the tank deck, there was a problem. It was one huge pile of junk. The tank deck was 200 feet long, 40 feet wide, and had an overhead of 20 feet. To handle the material aboard ship, we had two forklifts, neither of which was very large. A forklift can only lift palletized materials to the top of its rack, and no farther. Most of the material was not palletized. A passageway wide enough for a forklift was maintained through the middle of the tank-deck. On either side was open storage, with no shelves, no partitions, no bins, no nothing.

In the hustle to get material aboard the ship, the only record of what was aboard was a single checkmark on the load list by each item we had received, and nobody knew where on the tank deck anything was located. This was the story when I assumed responsibility for the Supply Department. As a minesweeper tender, a supply ship, we knew what we had, but it might take several days to find it. I found myself, uncomfortably, agreeing with the captain. Was this really a supply ship? I retrieved my three little steel balls, and started my own routine. Clack, clack, clack, clack went the three little balls.

For the next eighteen months, the storekeepers had one simple assignment, beyond their usual responsibilities. We needed to set up a locator system for the items we had aboard, then inventory all the items and show where, on the tank deck, each item was stored. We took inventory for eighteen months, and added where it was on the tank deck.

As a matter of great curiosity, I examined the load list of gear that was supposed to be aboard the Hamilton County. One of the descriptors for each item was the volume required for storage. With a Marchant calculator, I totaled the volumes for all the items on the list, and discovered the complete load list of items would have filled the tank deck three times stacked solidly. It was clearly a load list from hell, and it was all mine. We had no idea if we had "all the important stuff".

WOODEN SHIPS: IRON MEN

Unlike many of my courses in Naval Science, the classes on Naval Warfare were the most fascinating. With advancing science, the weapons of modern warfare were becoming technically interesting. The technology used in mines was also fascinating. Unlike older mines that detonated on contact, newer mines had sensors that could gauge the size or proximity of ships passing nearby, and detonate only when the proper signal configuration was achieved. Others mines might count the ships passing overhead, and detonate only after a predetermined number of passes had been recorded. These mines were all invisible from the surface without special detection devices.

In wartime, minefields could be laid out along coastal waters, harbors or rivers to discourage the passage of ships. Blockade of a harbor could be achieved with mines alone. As passive devices, mines remain submerged well after hostilities end, and pose serious threats to commerce until they are cleared from the waterways. Clearing mines was the task of the minesweepers, a small vessel tailored for the job.

The Hamilton County was a minesweeper tender designed to provide support for an assortment of minesweepers. By January 1956 when I reported aboard, the Navy had developed a minesweeper which had all the bells and whistles needed to sweep mines and avoid being blown up in the process. The following picture shows three sweepers, the Warbler (MSC-206), the Widgeon (MSC-208), and a third sweeper alongside the

Hamilton County well prior to our deployment to the Western Pacific. The ships had only been in service for a few months, and had the latest in minesweeper warfare technology. Most of the sweepers and the Hamilton County were subsequently home-ported in Sasebo, where they served the Navy's needs for the next 15 years. They were the cats whiskers in minesweepers at the time.

These sweepers originated the popular notion of wooden ships and iron men. The ships were designed to present a minimum magnetic signal, compared with metal hull ships. Their engines and associated equipment were built with non-magnetic alloys wherever possible. Degaussing cable was used to neutralize the magnetic influence that could not be elimin-ated. For example, consumable goods in tin cans were stored in permanent places aboard ship. After they were used, the cans were washed, returned to the original boxes, and placed on the same storage shelves to avoid altering the ships magnetic char-acteristics. When the cooks failed to follow these rather expli-cit instructions, the result could blow the ship out of the water. This made the ships cooks extraordinarily attentive.

With their dangerous mission, it was essential that the ships, hulls, and all onboard equipment be tested for the ability to withstand water-born explosions, as may occur while actually sweeping for mines. As the flagship for minesweepers, the Ham-ilton County was to oversee the testing.

To prepare for testing, we loaded a dozen yellow mines on

the main deck, ordered the helicopter to come aboard, and for the first and only time in a year and a half, the Admiral, Commander Mine Forces Pacific Fleet, came aboard with his staff to witness the testing. Once everything and everybody was aboard, we left for a remote island in the Catalina group off Southern California. As we were steaming into Catalina, the below picture shows the dozen yellow mines waiting to be used, the HUP-2 helicopter strapped to the deck, and Catalina Island dead ahead of the ships bow. We were about to find out exactly how sea worthy these little wooden ships and their iron men would be.

We anchored in a large protected cove to begin preparation for the testing. It was never quite clear exactly how the one minesweeper (MSC) designated for the testing was selected from among many. The admiral may well have asked for volunteers. Had they known that the crew would be aboard the ship as the mines were detonated, they might have had second thoughts about volunteering. As most MSC captains were Annapolis graduate JGs, they may have stood in line for the honor. In any event, one minesweeper and many of its crew were all aboard, at anchor a considerable distance from the admiral and the rest of us on the Hamilton County when the fireworks began.

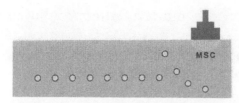

The above is a schematic of the minesweeper (MSC) at anchor, while the yellow circles represent the mines placed at various distances and depths from the ship. Testing required the better part of a day, beginning early in the morning. Initially the most distant mine was detonated. Following each detonation, the crew on the minesweeper would check the ship for damage, making special note of anything that might be moved by the shock. The initial explosion may have been 150 yards from the ship and 30 feet below the surface.

After the ship was checked, the next nearer mine was detonated, and the routine was repeated. This went on throughout the day until all twelve mines had been detonated. The last few charges were designed to provide a lateral shock to the side (abeam) of the ship, and the final blast was almost below the ship's hull, providing vertical thrust.

By and large, the remote explosions did little more than produce waves and a rocking motion commonly experienced by everything that floats. From about 50 yards and closer, items that were not securely fastened to the ship were moved by the jolt, but the little wooden ship was amazingly sturdy. The final few jolts were extraordinary in their impact on both the wooden ship and the iron men, with the men being the more resilient. On visual during the final explosion, the little ship appeared to be raised about four feet above its former waterline before settling back into the water.

There was no major damage to the wooden hull of the ship, although the main engines were reportedly knocked loose from their shipyard alignments. Virtually everything that could be moved, jostled, or knocked over, was moved, jostled, or knocked over. After a brief period of adjustment by the iron men, the little ship returned from the testing site on its own power. Their sea worthiness was beyond question following this brutal series of tests.

The test was not without its surprising outcome. The first detonations produced almost no visible consequences. The last few explosions produced hundreds of stunned fish in the cove. When the testing was over, the LCVP used to move men and equipment during the test was used to gather in the fish that had been stunned. For the better part of a half hour, the crew of the LCVP gathered fish until the bottom of the boat was covered with fish. Then it returned to the Hamilton County. The following picture shows the admiral on his only stay aboard the Hamilton County (left) and Captain Weatherby (right) struggling to hold two of the larger three fish which were captured in the exercise. The brightly colored black and orange fish, I was told, is a sheep's head, while the larger gray-brown fish is a sea bass.

Because the cooks on the ship reported to me first, they asked if I would like some of the sea bass to take home. I said a small portion would be fine, enough for two meals. They filleted about two pounds and froze it for taking home. This was a fitting and delicious end of our testing. The fish was great and the wooden ships were amazing, but the iron men had earned their name and their reputation.

THE WARDROOM RAT

There was never any dispute about the infestation of rats aboard the Hamilton County. My primary concern was that the critters leave their droppings away from the fresh fruit and vegetables, and far removed from the food storage areas. Garbage was a serious problem, as a little bit can attract rats for miles around. The cooks never acknowledged any problems. As nocturnal animals, most of the sightings were at night, when they were hungry, thirsty, or looking for a willing female. Like all good sailors, they did their best work after dark.

As becomes the custom aboard ship, when you can't sleep or otherwise have nothing to do, what you do is drink coffee until something happens. Particularly at 0300 in the morning, when you are awake and underway at sea, there is absolutely nothing worthwhile to do. The coffee mess is never far away. Such was the case on the Hamilton County. Even bad coffee can become a serious habit, when steaming in a straight line for several days in a row. "Turn to: Continue ship's work" is the traditional announcement piped over the ship's public address system right after lunch. It breaks the monotony, and awakens the sailors from short luncheon naps. After working hours, the monotony is rarely broken.

Aboard ship there are noises everywhere. The bow-wake is the most pleasant, if it can be heard over the muffled engine noise from the ship's stack. In a reasonable sea, a metal ship twists and turns, creaks and cracks, and scrapes and pounds. On rare occasions the sea is so calm a seasoned sailor is unable to sleep at all. There are few noises to lull him to sleep. This was one of those occasions. The Pacific was so calm as we steamed toward the Orient, that there was not a single ripple on the surface of the ocean, a sea of glass. It was this way for several days. A wave here or there helps break the monotony.

Given this void of stimuli, I found myself drinking coffee in the wardroom early in the morning. Reading a magazine required turning a page every now and then. That was the only sound that broke the silence of the wardroom. Then it seemed like I was no longer alone. I thought I heard a faint rustle from the food preparation area in the next compartment. I looked toward the opening in the bulkhead through which food was delivered to the wardroom. I saw nothing. I scanned the buffet used for storing silver and serving utensils just this side of the opening. I saw nothing. The rustling continued on and off. I would hear the rustling, but when I looked, I saw nothing. This went on for several minutes. Then finally I saw a small gray-brown head with two little ears sticking up over the back of the buffet.

"Avast, ye landlubber" I hollered, and the furry varmint ducked back behind the buffet. At about that moment, Ensign John Pursley, from the great state of Indiana arrived. Clearly, I needed reinforcements to rid the wardroom of this scavenger. There was only one exit from the wardroom, so I asked John to block the door, and we would get some weapons of mass destruction for the job. The only weapons available were a broom and a mop handle hanging on the bulkhead down the passageway. We got both, mindful to keep the intruder trapped in the wardroom.

Then through deft and cunning, we coaxed the intruder from behind the buffet and into the open. Initially we only grazed him with glancing blows, scaring the by-golly out of him. Then we adjusted our sights and managed a few direct hits. Fortunately, we were reinforced once again by the chief master at arms, who arrived with a fire axe. Among the three of us, we were able to administer repeated blows until the rat staggered and fell without ever leaving the wardroom. The next morning there appeared on the wardroom bulletin board a proclamation in the Navy's finest official jargon. It was unsigned, because the SPCA can appear at any moment, even in the Navy. It read as follows:

U.S.S. Hamilton County (LST-802)

c/o Fleet Post Office

San Francisco, California

PROCLAMATION

BE IT PROMULGATED THAT ON THE EVENING OF 16 OCTO-BER 1956 WHILE SHOOTING CRAPS IN THE WARDROOM, THE ACE RAT SPOTTER FROM COMRATPAC, TAD ABOARD THE HAM-ILTON COUNTY, DID SPOT AND UPON CONFERRING WITH THE CRACK RAT KILLER FROM THE HOOSIER STATE (ALSO TAD FROM COMRATPAC) DID CONSPIRE AGAINST SAID SPOTTED RAT.

ARMED WITH THE LATEST COMRATPAC ANTI-RAT EXTER-MINATORS (I.E. ONE BROOM AND ONE MOP HANDLE) THE COURAGEOUS TEAM DID CAPTURE SAID SPOTTED RAT (NOW THE CAPTURED RAT) AND MAINTAINED SAID RAT THUS UNTIL THE ARRIVAL OF THE CHIEF MASTER AT ARMS WHO, WITH A FIRE AX, DID CONFER BLOWS TO SAID CAPTURED RATS HEAD AND EARS CAUSING DEATH.

THE HAMILTON COUNTY EXTENDS ITS APPRECIATION TO THE COURAGEOUS TEAM FROM COMRATPAC FOR EXTER-MINATING THE WARDROOM RAT AND DISCOURAGING FUR-THER ENTRANCE OF OTHER UNAUTHORIZED RATS INTO THE WARDROOM.

BE IT SO PROMULGATED!

Bob Settles

HONOLULU HANG-UP

The Hamilton County's new mission as a minesweeper tender started six months before I reported aboard. All prescribed minesweeper and helicopter supplies that could be loaded aboard were stored and accounted for. We spent a few days in San Diego testing the integrity of a wooden hulled minesweeper by trying to blow it out of the water. We couldn't. We stocked up on stores and provisions needed for a long tour. As soon as a full complement of officers and men was aboard, we steamed out of Long Beach for the Western Pacific. This was the ship's first tour as a minesweeper tender to the combat zones of the far east. We left Long Beach in the late summer of 1956 with a short stop planned for Honolulu, a convenient liberty port in route to Sasebo, Japan.

LSTs are not noted for their dashing good looks, and they wallow from port to port at a top speed of 10 knots with a tail wind and following seas. The first leg of our journey from Long Beach to Honolulu was 2,226 nautical miles, a distance covered by today's jets in four hours. By contrast, our journey boggled the imagination. Averaging nine knots per hour, a straight line to Honolulu was predicted to take 247 hours, a hair over ten days travel time. After a few days steaming, the line from the old song I'd love to get you on a slow boat to China, took on an entirely new meaning. As there were only sailors on the ship, we had all been got, as we were on the ship by ourselves. It was peaceful, pleasant, ponderous, and painful making this first overseas journey.

After the tenth full day of steaming in a straight line, we were elated to arrive in Honolulu for two days of rest and recreation. We tied-up alongside a pier in Pearl Harbor, and anticipated making the most of a short, but relaxing visit on Oahu's Waikiki Beach. The liberty parties were well prepared, and few died in the rush to get off the gangway as they left the ship. Liberty on Oahu was all it was expected to be, a great break from steaming in a straight-line hour after hour. Little did we know at the time that thoroughly scurrilous forces were at work aboard the ship. We were soon to find out.

About noon of the second day in Pearl Harbor, the most startling news was reported. The chief engineer, who was responsible for the ship's propulsion, reported that some iron filings had been found in one of the main engine's oil filters. For this reason, he said, it was essential that a thorough examination of the engine be performed. The source of the filings had to be established beyond any doubt. He further explained to Captain Weatherby and others that the engine could not be run at all until it was given a clean bill of health.

Exactly how long it might take to examine the engine thoroughly was not known. The engine involved was huge, sitting eight feet in height and fifteen feet long in the ships starboard-side engine room. While its size was not a major problem, examining the engine thoroughly might require complete disassembly until the origin of the metal filings could be found. Once the source was found, the solution would depend upon the findings. This was the theory on which we were operating.

The crew was divided into two duty sections, and each duty section was given liberty on alternate days until the ship was again seaworthy. So here we were, stranded on a tropical island, a few miles from Honolulu and Waikiki Beach for some indeterminate period of time. The crew was alternately shocked and delighted by this startling turn of events. Grudgingly, they took turns visiting Waikiki Beach, enjoying the white sand and the view of Diamond Head as it looked in 1956.

Our trying situation was the subject of considerable speculation aboard ship. We had been steaming at a steady speed in a straight line for ten continuous days, and throughout that period, the engines performed perfectly. The oil filters remained clean and pure. On arrival the engines were shut down and liberty was started. Only on the second day, the day before we were to resume our journey, did the iron filings appear. Voila! The timing of the iron filings was magnificent. None of us had any reason for suspicion, so we simply relaxed, enjoyed the liberty, and the fresh breezes of Oahu.

Each day that followed, the chief engineer reported that their examination was proceeding on schedule. Each day he reported that they had not found anything to explain the iron filings. This pattern of reports, and liberty, reports, and liberty continued for ten days. Throughout this period, we were struggling from day to day, not knowing what to expect. It was a grueling experience.

Finally, the engineer announced that the engine had been completely disassembled, each part examined under a microscope, and the source of the suspicious iron filings could not be found. The only thing left to do was to reassemble the engine, and hope they had not overlooked anything. One more day in port, he said, and we should be able to resume our trip to Sasebo. That was the way it happened.

We all knew the engineer was an officer and gentleman. He was a person of impeccable integrity. He inspired the same qualities among all the men in his division. At the same time, the ships stewards, who reported to me, often knew things about certain officers and men from monitoring their personal living spaces. One of the stewards reported that he had seen a small cup of iron shavings in the Chief Engineers stateroom. He was not exactly sure when he had first noticed these shavings, whether it was before or after we arrived in Hawaii. He also reported that he had experienced some wonderful liberty on the island. As he grinned from ear to ear, I decided to let his story die a natural death.

Being nicely refreshed, we resumed our slow float to Sasebo. A distance of 3,045 nautical miles, it was destined to consume 14 more days steaming in a straight line. For some reason, not a single complaint was heard about the second part of our journey. The trip originally expected to take 27 days actually took 36, just over 10% of an entire year. Because of the wasted travel time, the Hamilton County's homeport was changed to Sasebo, Japan shortly after we arrived in the Orient, eliminating for all time the possibility of another Honolulu hang-up.

We were all thoroughly refreshed from our ten days of surprise liberty in Oahu. Anyone aboard the ship might have harbored a small cup of iron filings, ignorant of their potential value. The chief engineer knew exactly what to do with them, proving the amazing power of a few iron shavings when placed in the hands of an expert. We never knew if the iron shavings really came from the engines oil filter. As it turned out, nobody even cared.

CONTRAST IN
CULTURES

With orders to report for independent duty as the Supply Officer on the Hamilton County (LST-802) in the winter of 1955, Lois and I moved to Long Beach, California, the ship's home port. Almost simultaneously I received a promotion to LTJG, and bright new stripes for my dress uniforms, a badge of honor that I was no longer a boot ensign. Fortunately for me, I received my additional half-stripe before locking horns with the captain of the ship, or I might never have seen the light of day again.

Following a few adjustments for its new mission as a Minesweeper Tender, we received orders to head for Sasebo, Japan. Pearl Harbor was our first stop in route, where we encountered some iron filings in a filter of one of the ship's main engines. Except for the men in the Engineering Department, this unfortunate event forced us all into unrestricted liberty in Honolulu and Waikiki Beach for ten days. This repair time, plus our dashing speed of 10 knots while underway, consumed almost six weeks for us to arrive in Sasebo. This delay and transit time was viewed with some distress by those in authority, and the ship had its home port changed to Sasebo, Japan for the duration. No more trips would be required through Hawaii, and no more chance collections of iron filings could be discovered as soon as we tied-up alongside the dock in Pearl Harbor.

An automatic byproduct of this decision made it legal for wives and families of the sailors to live in Sasebo. While government housing was not available for dependents, a fair number of sailors actually took advantage of this new arrangement, and flew their wives into Japan for a hearty taste of the Far East.

Just ten years after the end of WWII, Japan was still honoring most of her traditional and cultural trappings. For those from the United States, the time-honored traditions of the Japanese people were something to behold. When meeting on the streets, Japanese acquaintances would bow to 90 degrees as a sign of respect. The wives walked through the streets two or three paces behind their husbands. If packages were carried, the wives carried them.

The time-honored tradition of husbands spending one evening a week in the company of a Geisha was unquestioned, although the services provided by a Geisha were vastly different from those associated with call girls. At the same time, prostitution was fully legal, and for several miles surrounding each Navy base, the bars and night clubs featured signs advertising their beautiful and willing young ladies. On entering such establishments, the unattached ladies might form a circle or a line, expecting you to examine each in turn, and select the one that tickles your fancy. It was a bachelor's paradise, featuring both immediate gratification and hidden perils that could appear suddenly or insidiously a few hours or days following such visits.

After setting up housekeeping in a private residence, and becoming familiar with the Sasebo surroundings, we started exploring the country side. Nagasaki was only an hour's train ride south of Sasebo, so we booked fare to Nagasaki for a day of sightseeing. As everyone at the time knew, Nagasaki was the target of the second atomic bomb. Memories of the bombing were still fresh in all the minds, and actually visiting the site was high on our list of priorities. Of course, our memories and the memories of the residents of Nagasaki were vastly different.

One of our first visits was to the home of Madam Butterfly. Her romantic hideaway was beautifully perched on a hill-top overlooking Nagasaki Bay and the shipyards, which were the actual target of the bombing. As it turned out, the bomb was dropped more than a mile off target to the north, leaving Madam Butterfly's home and the shipyards undamaged. The mushroom cloud erupted over a strictly residential area in a valley near a newly constructed Catholic Church. It was a beautiful, red brick structure only a few hundred yards from the blast center, and except for a few reinforced columns and corner structures around the bell-tower, it was totally destroyed. The rubble had been cleared, but the front tower ruin was preserved as a historic relic for viewing by tourists. Looking down into the valley from the church ruins, we could see a peace statue in a small park at the precise center of the detonation. The surrounding homes had been rebuilt in the valley along a perfect grid of square blocks and straight streets with an underground sewage system, unlike that seen in any other city in Japan.

Madame Butterfly's home overlooking shipyards that were intended target in Nagasaki

Shipyard as viewed from Madame Butterfly's garden across the bay

Nagasaki's peace museum with re-
pository of blast relics

Actual blast center in residential area of Nagasaki

Charred remnants of church that was
new, but in the blast center

Peace statue located at the blast center in Nagasaki

Buddhist shrine with ceremonial bibs on small statues

One of the local haunts for sailors in Sasebo

Home away from home on second story
of private home in Sasebo

From the church we went to the small park preserved at the blast center where the large statue was displayed. The statue was of a person with one arm raised with the index finger pointing toward the sky. The other arm was outstretched horizontally to the side with the hand positioned parallel with the ground. A nearby plaque contained a detailed description of the symbolism included in the design of the statue, a wish for peace. From my perspective no symbolism was needed for this turning point in a war. The arm extended toward the sky points to the blast center, and the horizontal arm displays the result. In other words, the bomb came from above, and flattened everything you can see. War is hell.

Our final visit was to the Peace Center, a museum which displayed much of the memorabilia from the bombing experience. It showed garments discolored by the heat and radiation from the blast, straw embedded in solid bricks, and glass fused into rock-like structures. Prominently displayed were copies of leaflets and fliers dropped by American pilots a day or two before the bombing advising the population to leave the city in order to avoid death or serious injury. It was reported that the authorities would not allow the people to leave the city in response to the notice, resulting in far more casualties and injuries than necessary.

The last stop before leaving the Peace Center was a badly

needed visit to the public facilities, the restroom. It was located just off the large atrium on the ground floor. While Lois and I were both in need, Lois' need was approaching acute. The facility featured only a single door, and displayed the usual entry sign in Japanese. Lois sought confirmation that this was the place for both men and women, and was assured that it was. Lois appealed to me to accompany her through the single-door entryway. I declined her request, assuring her in the process that there are just some things in life you must do by yourself. Finally, she entered on her own, achieving an experience she has found necessary to describe on many subsequent occasions.

To her dismay and distress, the single door opened up into a huge, unisex restroom. It was designed to accommodate both men and women with equal facility, featuring no booths or partitions for privacy for the tasks to be accomplished therein. Neither did it feature any porcelain facilities for sitting while achieving. Rather it displayed, in open air for all to see, a series of holes in the floor along the walls over which one could assume the proper posture. There were no facilities for leaning, resting, or grab bars to assist with one's descent to or ascent from the holes in the floor, requiring that one innovate and balance as needed. Those unaccustomed to such low-rise facilities were called upon to exercise muscles and achieve movements not entirely within one's repertoire.

She surveyed this situation carefully, and never having witnessed such a facility as this in her previous 23 years, she puzzled over exactly how she should proceed. As she was wearing a long, tight skirt, high heels, a girdle with fasteners for long hose, and long hose, she knew that the experience would be a painful and protracted affair. With her light skin, she was certain that the surrounding patrons would thoroughly enjoy watching her wrestle with her attire to accomplish her mission.

When compared with his and hers facilities, partitioned private booths with porcelain seating fixtures in the United States,

Lois was certain that this personal experience would become life's most embarrassing moment. Unfortunately, nature's call can be delayed only so long, so she took the plunge. The emotional overlay was matched equally by the physical feat she was challenged to achieve in the process.

Precisely, the physical challenge she describes as having to pull a very long, straight skirt up to the waist, in order to pull the girdle and hose clear down to the ankles, while balancing on high spike heels all the time. Following these maneuvers, she must then assume the position sufficiently centered above the hole in the floor without the assistance of grab bars, and maintain this position for the duration. The entire act would challenge the skills of an accomplished acrobat, and was on display for all to see.

As she emerged from the facility, there could be little doubt that she had lowered herself to the occasion, perched perilously with perfect poise, and performed in such a fashion as to raise no suspicion at all. From the look on her face, she survived the unisex toilet relieved, unscathed and undamaged, except for the emotional scars from the anticipation.

In what appeared to be an anticlimax, she succeeded in her mission, and was shocked to discover that nobody in the facility even seemed to acknowledge that she was there. The Japanese tradition of extreme politeness was a surprise byproduct of her restroom experience, as nobody looked, she thinks, while she was so busy.

The return trip to Sasebo on the train was uneventful, which Lois enjoyed in complete comfort. Because I had refused to enter such an undifferentiated facility, I thereby deprived myself of one of the cultural thrills from our many months enjoying Japan.

TYPHOON T

One of the Hamilton County's trips out of Sasebo was to Subic Bay in the Philippines. In the fall of 1956, we arrived in Subic, anchored out for tendering ashore, and spent a few days of R and R touring the island of Luzon. Subic Bay included a naval repair facility adjoining Olongapo, our point of entry. From there we made a quick trip to Clarke Air Base where we understood the base exchange was outstanding. In route to and from Clarke, a flavor of the tropical culture was clearly evident. The landscape was dotted with rusted tanks and other remains of the war, which was only a decade old.

One of my first views was of a farmer's home built upon stilts that held it ten feet above the valley floor. Under the shelter of the house he had parked his ford tractor. Except for this one tractor, the entire agricultural economy seemed to depend upon the water buffalo. There were thousands of water buffaloes. They were in the fields, in the ponds, and throughout the hills and valleys. The buffaloes were not only beasts of burden, they were also the primary source of transportation for the local farmers.

The farmer above is riding to or from market while towing his family on a rustic wagon, pulled by his water buffalo, of course. Rice paddies fill the valley in the background. His wagon features solid round wheels. Special note should be made of the fresh mud on his wheels, which is eight inches deep at one point. The iron ring around the outside of each wheel protects the solid inside, which otherwise might break apart. The round mold ridge that surrounds the axle suggests the wheels might be poured concrete. Concrete would be quite heavy, but would withstand the moisture of the tropical climate, and deep mud in every field in the area. The concrete highway surface holds the family high and dry for this stretch of their trip.

When water buffalo are not working in the fields, they were usually found resting in water. The story is that water buffalo have no sweat glands in their hide, and as a result, are unable to cool themselves as efficiently as other beasts of burden. For this reason, they may only work for short periods of time, before they must cool down from the accumulated heat. The buffalo below are nicely immersed in cooling water. They may have served their time and are in the cool-down phase, or they may be waiting their turn to work the rice paddies. Both are tethered to the wooden trestle of the bridge.

After a few days at anchor in Subic Bay, we learned that a typhoon was approaching from the east of Luzon, and would be hazardous to our health if we remained in the protected harbor. There would be nothing more embarrassing than for our T to be blown up onto the bank in a high wind, and remain there as a permanent monument. With the Ts high freeboard, a strong wind abeam would blow it like a feather in a whirlwind. We deemed it advisable to get out of town as soon as possible. As our essential business had been completed, there was nothing to keep us in port.

Heading back for Sasebo, we were partially sheltered for two days by the island of Luzon, which moderated the typhoons winds. The seas were substantial, and the wind was steady from dead ahead at 50 to 60 knots or better. Steaming north along the coast of Luzon, we were within sight of land continuously, except when the rain was so heavy that it obscured our view. Believing that there was no reason to change course, we continued our heading straight north. With our blazing cruising speed of 10 knots, we believed it impossible to run into the more dangerous portion of the storm. So, we continued steady on course. It was often possible to take a fix on certain landmarks, as a benchmark for gauging our progress to the north. The first day we made considerable headway, averaging five knots per hour, or about 125 miles for 24 hours of steaming. As we approached the open seas north of Luzon, the sea became exceedingly heavy from dead ahead. The waves averaged 25-35 feet from trough to swell. At full power throughout the second day, we averaged one to two knots of headway each hour, and traveled fewer than thirty knots the second day. We were steaming at full power, yet we were going nowhere. While we were making almost no headway, it was far safer to head into the seas than to turn around with following seas. Had we turned around, with the high winds and following sea, we could have made Australia in record time.

An LST is constructed over a honeycomb of small compartments, each of which is watertight. Many can carry fuel oil, a few can hold aviation gas, and when empty, they can be filled with water for ballast, or left empty. Because of this structure, Ts are virtually unsinkable unless the ship was to break apart. This thought passed through our minds as we continued straight into the typhoon's headwinds.

Our experience from these first two days was not very comforting. The ship was taking a continual pounding. As the bow would break over the crest of a wave and move over the trough, it would hang over open space until the water reached the ship's center of gravity. Then the bow would drop precipitously, hitting the water with its flat bottom with such force that the entire ship would vibrate like a giant string, which had just been plucked. The noise was startling, and the splash created by the bow was awesome. Standing near the superstructure looking forward, the vibration could be observed at about three waves per second, and lasted for several seconds. After two days of continuous pounding, we started to notice stress fractures in the steel of the main deck, immediately above the tank deck. The first sign of this damage was water that leaked through the cracks, dripping or running onto the tank deck twenty feet below. There was little that could be done at the time, so we continued our ponderous northward course.

The third day was the worst, as we finally reached the open ocean north of Luzon. By that time, we were quite accustomed to the pounding and the vibration that followed. There was little work being performed aboard ship during this period, except on the bridge. If any of the sailors were seasick, it was not readily apparent. Most of the crew spent little time in the mess hall, often a sign that they are not feeling well. The tables in the mess hall and the wardroom were fully equipped with side-rails to prevent the meal-trays from sliding off the tables. Stores that were stacked in the storerooms all came tumbling over. Tables, chairs, and any furniture, which was not fastened permanently to the steel decks, migrated to the nearest fixed obstruction. Captain Weatherby and his crew of sailors proved their expertise, steering us straight into the headwinds for three straight days. Finally, the typhoon passed beyond our little T, and we wallowed like a giant cork on into Sasebo. The Secretary of Defense, Don Rumsfeld, would readily classify this particular ocean voyage as a world-class nail-biter.

By far the worst ride of the trip was experienced by the crew, whose living quarters were along both sides of the ship from the superstructure to the bow, one level below the main deck. Those living in the compartments farthest forward described it like riding a bucking bronco in slow motion. The differences were in amplitude of the motions. The bow would first move up 20 to 30 feet over several seconds, then drop suddenly until it reached the trough 20 to 30 feet below. On striking the water, there was a loud noise which carried throughout the ship, and a jolt as it stopped on the flat bottom. This jolt then initiated the vibration through several cycles. This routine was repeated every 20 to 30 seconds, depending on the distance between swells.

The physical experience in the rack produced increased weight or gravity as the bow is elevated, and you are pressed deeply into the mattress. Then there is a transition from increased weight to reduced weight, as the bow begins its descent to the trough. On reaching the bottom, there is a pounding jolt, and a loud noise which accompanies the jolt. The vibration follows the jolt for a second or two. Then the cycle is repeated, over and over. You can only imagine what it is like trying to sleep through such gyrations. A few could not sleep at all, and moved to the stern of the ship, where the ride was slightly more comfortable. This describes only the physical motions, and in no way can account for the acute misery of those few who experienced sea-sickness as an added bonus.

On arrival in Sasebo, we staggered off the ship, relieved to be home at last, and plant our feet on something that was not pounding and vibrating. A preliminary inspection of the ship showed 27 fractures in the steel plates of the main deck. One of the cracks was sufficiently wide to see daylight from the tank deck below. An equal number of cracks were found around the hull, suggesting that a complete inspection and repair was required. We were moved immediately into dry dock where the keel was blocked-up and the water pumped out. The Hamilton County was high and dry for the better part of ten days, while we patched and repaired the damage created by the typhoon.

The ship was nicely repaired following those three days of pounding, and seemed none the worse for the wear. By contrast, our brains were left with a permanent etching of this harrowing, three-day ordeal.

CUMSHAW NAVY

For dozens of good official reasons, the Hamilton County had its homeport changed from Long Beach, California to Sasebo, Japan shortly after we arrived in Westpac in the fall of 1956. This may have been to avoid the two months transit time across the pacific each year, or possibly to keep honorable sailors from pouring iron filings in the main engines on each trip through Hawaii. This latter trick offers ten days of unexpected liberty at Waikiki Beach on each crossing. While such nefarious tricks may be commonplace in the Navy, officially changing the homeport to Sasebo controls only a few tricks. It also sets in motion an entirely new set of unofficial incentives and priorities that are weighed carefully by the crew. Whenever you mess with the minds of sailors, it is important to post a careful watch. With the watch posted, it is interesting to know who-all were active participants in these unofficial games.

The Hamilton County was a supply ship, and for better or worse, I was its supply officer. This did not make me quite God, but I did find myself close to him, – the captain. This relationship was never a smooth one from the day I reported aboard, and the captain questioned whether the Hamilton County was really a supply ship. The admiral of Mine Forces, Pacific Fleet had assured the Captain that I was fully responsible for the stores aboard the ship. This understanding was planted in a minefield, the captain's mind. I was not sure how many times the field had been smashed during his illustrious career.

As a product of submarine forces until 1955, Captain (Lt.) Vernon W. Weatherby, a mustang with a sixth-grade education, was thoroughly familiar with the system of accountability practiced in the underwater forces. There was either little or none. Most of the subs of the day did not have supply officers, as such, so when payday rolled around, for instance, they needed to find a ship with money, and a supply officer, to pay the crew to go on liberty. It was not a very efficient system, but the Navy had learned decades before that money lying around loose had a half-life of under a minute. Everything else that was not attached to the ship had a half-life somewhat longer. This is not an impeachment of the thoroughly honest and honorable men of the Navy. It is simply an acknowledgement that government property and personal possessions do not fit into the same category. One might guard personal possessions with a degree of vigor. As the ships supply officer, I discovered the crew did not guard my supplies with the same vigor they expended with their own stuff.

The notion of accountability was all that was missing. The captain, as the final authority aboard ship, believed that he had the last word. Unfortunately for me, the Bureau of Supplies and Accounts in Washington had me believing that I was responsible for the proper use and accounting for all my departments supplies aboard ship. I was thoroughly familiar with the stories of supply officers who ignored their warnings, and spent time in small cells in Leavenworth for their failings. I never heard of a single captain spending time in such a secure facility. Unfortunately for me, the captain was never able to master the concept of accountability, a notion for which he had no compartment.

The Supply Department had a ship full of valuable stores of all kinds, and a highly capable crew of sailors and men working for me. By contrast, the captain's navy, the one full of longstanding custom and hallowed tradition, also knew the ship was full of valuable stores of all kinds. This was McHale's Navy to which the captain subscribed. If we needed critical supplies, a jeep, or other valuables not within our immediate grasp, the process was to locate an item or items of comparable value, and exchange them for what you needed. It avoided all the paperwork and bother, otherwise required by the system. This system is called cumshaw, and might involve an exchange of equal values, or could be an outright gift in exchange for favors. My safe prevented an exchange of money for services, because it weighed 3,000 pounds, and was welded to the deck. Everything else was coveted by those with needs.

We had just come through a typhoon that produced about 50 cracks in steel plates in the hull, main deck, and other internal structures of the ship. Dry-dock was required to perform all the repairs. In dry-dock the ships main deck was oriented about a foot from a parallel walkway ashore. It was an easy reach over the main deck railing along the length of the ship. This made it convenient to transfer material from the shore to the ship, or visa-versa. The visa versa was the one of concern to me. The deck-watch was posted by the gangway near the stern to oversee the ships official carryings-on. The ships unofficial carryings-on were not handled through the deck watch at the stern.

After a day or so in dry-dock, I was pulled aside by the Chief Petty Officer on watch, who told me that one of my storekeepers had been seen, he believed, hustling a box of goods off the ship. He didn't know what was in the box, but it appeared to be quite heavy to carry. He had placed the goods on the walkway a considerable distance from the gangway. Then he walked off the gangway himself and back to the box, which he picked up and carried on off. The rest of the story, according to the CPO, was that the storekeeper, a bachelor, had an arrangement with one of the local honeys with whom he was shacking up every night. Given this critical piece of information, a motive, I suggested that he alert subsequent watches to keep a close eye on my storekeepers' goings and comings.

The following afternoon the deck watch caught him red handed with another box of goodies. I was called to the deck immediately where we examined the box and its contents. It was full of canned goods and other consumables required for house-keeping. He was reported to the captain for disciplinary action, as the captain might deem proper. Within a day or so, I was told the captain had seen the offender in his quarters, and was given a slap on the wrist. It was several days before I fully understood the captains rather feeble handling of this serious, second incident of theft.

With the ship resting high in dry-dock, it was possible to examine the hull thoroughly in detail. The work was started locating, buffing, welding, priming and painting all of the dozens of cracks where they were found. The deck was a wasteland of activity, and one that could hide a multitude of sins. With the compelling need to repair the ship, it was also a perfect opportunity to take full advantage of other shipboard needs while we were there. During the previous two years, a laundry list had been developed of all those things that somebody believed would make the ship a better place. For this reason, an additional list of repairs, modifications, improvements, upgrades, and enhancements was submitted through the chain of command for their consideration.

As is always the case, you never get everything you want through the bureaucracy, and some of the things scratched off the list are considered essential by shipboard authorities. Each department head has a little authority, but the Captain retains final authority for many shipboard issues. The captain pulls the strings, holds mast, kicks butt, and has the final say. Our particular captain was the byproduct of the submarine fleet, and based much of his action from his experience underwater, -where oxygen for thought may be rare.

To supervise the ship's repair, a civilian foreman was assigned to coordinate the shipyard authorities and workmen. In this middleman role, he dealt with the captain on a daily basis. He assured the captain that some of those things that had not been approved could probably be arranged for the proper consideration, – a little cumshaw. This understanding was outside of that given official sanction. And so, with this gentleman's agreement, all the shipboard work was well underway.

A day or so later, a cook pulled me aside for a conversation. It went like this:

"Mr. Settles", he said, "We need to talk in private".

"What is it, Charles?" I asked.

"Captain Weatherby called me up to his cabin a few days ago. He gave me a long list of things he said I should put in a box, and take to the foreman's office over on the dock."

"And what all was on the list?" I asked.

"It was mostly big food items," he replied.

"Do you have the list?" I asked.

"Yes," he said. "This is the list he gave me today."

"Is there more?" I asked.

"Yes. He gave me another list two days ago. I took those things to the foreman's office yesterday."

"Anything else?" I asked.

"Yes. When the captain tells you to do something, you can get your a__ in a crack if you don't do what he tells you to do."

"Charles," I said, "I appreciate you coming to me with this. Don't worry about it. You won't get into any trouble with the captain. If anybody hangs, I will be the first to go."

"Are you sure you can keep the captain off my case?" he asked.

"Don't worry about it, Charles. I will take care of Captain Weatherby. And welcome to Club Med," I added as an afterthought.

With this final assurance, the stage was nicely set for a meeting with the captain at his earliest opportunity. I knew, of course, that the meeting would be brutal, and would involve trying to wedge a concept into the captain's brain. I had tried to do this on numerous occasions in the past, and had failed miserably each time. The captain was ashore at the time, and was not expected to return until late in the evening. This delay afforded me time to choose among dozens of things I needed to say, knowing they would all be rejected.

When the captain returned, it was late evening. I was in the wardroom drinking coffee, where I had been most of the evening. It didn't help. As the two of us were alone in the wardroom, and the ship was deserted, we started.

"Good evening, Captain", I said.

"Hi, Bob", he replied.

"Help yourself to the coffee. I just made a fresh pot".

"Why are you here on the ship this evening?" he asked. "Your old lady is probably home waiting for you," he added.

"One of my men came to me this afternoon, and told me he was concerned about what you asked him to do. He gave me this list of provisions, and said he was supposed to collect them all, and take them to the foreman's office on the dock."

"Do you have a problem with that?" he asked.

"I have a serious problem with that." I answered. "I have to report to the Bureau of Supplies and Accounts on a regular basis about the status of the ships stores. This includes all the food on this list."

"Why haven't I seen any of these reports?" he asked.

"The Bureau requires that I report directly to them. The chain of command would require seven months for a report to arrive in Washington. Because I am personally responsible for accounting for all stores and money spent officially by the ship from my department, I am supposed to make a record of everything removed from my secured spaces."

"Since when are you responsible for the food on the ship?" he asked.

"The cooks all work for me, and they keep keys to all the food storage areas. We keep a running inventory of all the food aboard the ship. When somebody takes food from an area that is not recorded, I am held personally responsible for the loss."

"The cooks work for me, too, he replied, and I am the captain"

"Yes," I said, "But you are not personally responsible for the food, or anything else in my department. You are certainly not responsible for the money in my safe, are you?" I asked.

"No," he replied. "You are responsible for your safe and the money in it, he finally conceded."

"And I am fully responsible for everything else under my control in the department. Everything under lock and key in my department is my complete responsibility." I added.

"So, what did you tell Charles to do?" he asked.

"I told him the only thing I could tell him. I told him not to do what you had asked."

"You told him to disobey my order?" he asked.

"Yes, I did," I said.

"And on whose authority did you tell him not to obey my order?" he asked.

"The Bureau of Supplies and Accounts told me to," I answered.

"Did you call Washington about this?" he asked.

"No, I haven't called Washington, yet. At this point, it is really between just you and me. At the end of my tour on the Hamilton County, the bureau will audit my accounts, cash, food, stores, clothing, and all. If my records don't fully support my work, they give me an exception, and I can be held personally responsible for the value of any loss. This loss could come out of my personal funds."

"Since when does the Navy hold people personally responsible for things that are lost? I have never heard of anybody paying the Navy back," he said.

"Captain," I said, "the stuff on the list you gave to Charles was not lost. Had he taken it off the ship, like the box you sent yesterday, then it would be lost. It was in my storerooms. It was under my control, and my storekeepers have the keys. That is why Charles came to me."

"You know," the captain said, "that I have access to all your storerooms through an extra set of keys."

"Yes, I know you have access to all the ships spaces. If the ship catches fire, you need to get into every space for the safety of the ship," I said.

"And what keeps me from sending somebody into the frozen food locker for ice cream?" he asked.

It was at about this point that I took my hat from the table in the wardroom, and threw it across the room, hitting the outside bulkhead.

"Damn-it, Captain," I replied in total frustration, "If you think you need something out of one of my storerooms for official purposes, I want you to come straight to me, rather than going to one of my men and telling them to do something that is illegal. If you are willing to pay for the provisions you already sent ashore, I will see if we can work that out. I refuse to pay for what you have my men steal for you from my storerooms. If you can't restrain yourself from stealing, I will file a formal exception to your action up the chain of command, just so I don't have to pay for what you have my men steal."

"Just a minute now," he cautioned. "On the submarines, we did this kind of stuff all the time, and nobody said anything about it."

"Captain," I replied, "the Hamilton County is not a submarine. It is a minesweeper tender, a ship with a supply mission. I am its supply officer. I am responsible for the supplies aboard this ship. That is what the Admiral told you over the phone, didn't he?" I asked.

"Yes, he did say that," the captain replied.

"Because of this incident," I added, "I will be telling all the men in my department that they will issue stores and materials from supply department spaces only when they know I would approve it, – officially. I also intend to tell them that any request from you, or any other officer on the ship, must meet with my personal approval, over my signature."

With this, the captain stomped out of the wardroom.

The following evening, the officers from the ship had a party at the officers' club ashore. Wives and girlfriends were all in attendance. On one occasion, the captain pulled my wife aside for a private conversation.

"Lois," said the captain, "You need to have a long talk with your husband. He is out of control. He threw his hat across the wardroom the other night in a fit of anger. You should know that if he doesn't come home some evening, I may have him courts-martialed." She said the captain seemed to be exceedingly angry at the time.

When she told me about this conversation, she expressed concern that a court-martial was pretty serious stuff.

"Don't worry," I said. "The captain is far more concerned about the stuff he stole than my courts-martial. It is curious that he said this to you at a party, rather than to me in person."

This was the last I heard of stores being passed over the side of the ship. Seven years after leaving the Navy, I received notice that my accounts had been settled. The deficit following three years of service was over $7,000, much of which was over-issue of food items. The navy forgave me the debt without prejudice, for which I was grateful. It was an uphill battle against the old sailors, who had grown up in the cumshaw navy. As for Captain Weatherby, he never did find room for the notion of accountability in the constricted space between his ears.

SAYONARA US NAVY

Following my final run-in with the C.O., I elected to resign my regular commission in the Navy, and pursue my options in civilian life. As the ship was permanently stationed in Japan, all dependents overseas were entitled to return transportation to the continental U.S. at government expense. The papers identifying my intentions were signed, and we were listed for timely return transportation to the U.S. Shortly thereafter the Navy packed all our gear for shipment to Western Kansas, and we retained enough personal stuff to return to San Francisco where the papers separating me from active duty would be completed. My initial contract for active duty expired on June 7, 1957, and I anticipated that we would determine what course to pursue during a long summer on the Steeples farm near Palco, Kansas.

In late April we received orders providing concurrent travel via train to Tokyo and MSTS ship to San Francisco. Transportation to Tokyo was arranged on an overnight train with sleeping cars. The train's beds were somewhat short for sleeping comfortably, requiring sleeping with knees bent. The aroma of sushi saturated the train during the lunch hour, and the disposition of luncheon waste by throwing the remains directly onto the tracks through a hole in the middle of each train car was novel in our experience with trains. Most embarrassing was the drunken American sailors who so disrupted the dining car, that our dinner was delayed. Fortunately, I was traveling in civilian clothes, and did not find it necessary to personally intervene in the fracas with the sailors.

In preparation for leaving Japan, the below picture is a beautifully symbolic representation for all sailors who have strayed into and enjoyed Sasebo's harbor and Navy base. In the foreground is the USS Arnold J. Isbell (DD-869) outlined by what the sailors called Jane Russell Mountain, rising majestically in the background. This classic picture combines the power and spirit of the U.S. Navy and her many patriotic sailors, who had their hearts and minds in all the right places in the 1950s.

While waiting for the MSTS ship's arrival in Yokohama, we toured a few sights, and prepared to say a final farewell to the exotic and fascinating cultures of the Far East. When our ship arrived, we were packed and primed for the 10-11 day return cruise across the Pacific. As far as we could tell, the ship was booked full for the trip. The passengers were a cross section of all service personnel and dependents. The farewell party at the ship terminal in Yokohama was filled with thousands of emotional goodbyes and rivers of tears. The following picture was taken as we were 25 yards from the boarding facilities, stretching the streamers which appeared to anchor us to the dock as we began our slow entry into Tokyo Bay.

The first half day of steaming was peaceful, sunny, and pleasant. After a few hours underway from Japan the Pacific became characteristically rough, providing for most of the passengers their first experience riding a slow roll together with pitching and yawing. As stabilizers had not yet been invented for large ships, there was little that could be done to moderate the ship's motion. It was a bitter pill for a large number of passengers.

The ship was the equivalent in size of a Queen Mary with inside and outside cabins arranged along passageways on both port and starboard sides of the ship on several decks. Our particular cabin was one level below the main deck in the bow. This particular location is not ideal for experiencing your first ocean cruise, but Lois acquired her sea legs quite quickly, and without any of the serious byproducts that often accompany the first shipboard outing.

After the first night's steaming, we arose for breakfast, and trudged to the stern of the ship to the dining room. Along both port and starboard passageways, we noticed the hand rails were draped continuously with waxed-paper barf bags, – thousands of such bags. We ate breakfast, lounged a while, then returned to our cabin in the bow. We were shocked to discover that practically all of the bags had been removed from the railings, presumably based upon need. Clearly a very large number of passengers had succumbed to the motion of the ocean, and were undoubtedly hoping the motion would go away. For two or three days afterward, we saw relatively few persons enjoying the shipboard facilities, choosing instead to remain within the more comfortable confines of their cabins.

A few dozen hearty souls were unfazed by the experience, and were anxious to learn what options were available for passing the next ten days with little else to do. A fair number of couples were devoted bridge players, and we settled into playing bridge on and off through most of the journey. Slowly but surely, the formerly indisposed passengers gained their sea legs, and rejoined the living.

The ship sailed the great circle directly from Tokyo to San Francisco, and after dozens of rubbers of bridge and far too many meals, we arrived within sight of the Golden Gate Bridge. The sight of San Francisco was a culture shock following ten months in Japan. Japanese residential communities at the time consisted of one and two story, wood frame homes with paper partitions, glass enclosed patios, and winding, hilly streets with few street lights connecting them all together. It appeared to lack any sort of organization or advance planning. It was random in appearance, informal, and comfortable.

On coming within sight of San Francisco, the city was completely high-rise brick apartments with a whitewashed façade along straight streets and square blocks. It was formal, impersonal, and cold in appearance when compared with Japan. We docked not far from Fisherman's Wharf, and prepared for being transported to Treasure Island. On reporting at Treasure Island we were advised that government quarters were not available, and we would need to arrange for private quarters for an indefinite duration.

Because this was temporary duty pending separation, we were entitled to generous extra compensation to pay the cost of housing, meals, transportation, and incidentals. We were able to rent a small furnished apartment in San Francisco. Because my final separation papers had not been received, I was assigned to temporary duty with Lt. A.M. Scott, the officer charged with separating or discharging all Navy personnel who process through San Francisco. I was thoroughly familiar with the Navy's paper shuffling, and fit in with the task readily. From 8:00am till 5:00pm Monday through Friday, I signed papers discharging sailors through the facility on Treasure Island. It was a thankless and routine job, but provided something to do during the day, and generated a lucrative cash-flow to support the extended celebration of our return to the states.

From 5:00pm till 8:00am the next morning on week days, and all week end, Lois and I were free to explore every aspect of the San Francisco environment and surroundings. As we had no idea how long our temporary duty would last, every night was tailored to explore the jazz music venues, on-stage entertainment sites, and locally popular restaurants. We had stored an old car with Lois' aunt in Heyward while overseas, so bay area transportation was not an issue. With the encouragement of a healthy cash flow, we visited a Pontiac Dealer in Walnut Creek where we purchased a new 1957 Pontiac Hardtop, one of the hottest vehicles to come off the assembly line.

While we had no actual agenda, I expected that I would be separated by my final release date. We celebrated without restraint. Finally, June 7 came and went, yet there was no sign of my official release authorization from the Secretary of the Navy. As I was being compensated handsomely, it was not particularly distressing. Subsequently I learned that the Secretary of the Navy, Charles S. Thomas, was on maneuvers somewhere in the Atlantic, and was unable to process the proper papers until his return to the states and his office in Washington D.C.

For six weeks or longer, we examined every club, restaurant, and entertainment venue in the San Francisco area. These visits included a dive where Oscar Peterson was the featured entertainer in the middle of a small arena with smoke so thick as to make it uninhabitable. We laughed at the Smothers Brothers at the Hungry Eye, and we ate at the Domino Club which featured nude photographs along all the walls. An early introduction to the sexual revolution surrounding San Francisco was a dinner-show featuring Juan Jose, a male cross dresser who performed on stage as a female, undistinguishable from any other finely-shaped female. He tucked his long hair into a beret to walk the streets during the day. We ate on Fisherman's Wharf, toured Yosemite, walked through Stanford University and Palo Alto, admired the 19 mile drive along the Monterrey coast, watched the seals on the cliffs, ate dinner at the Cliff House Restaurant, amazed at the Golden Gate Bridge, visited Muir Woods and the giant redwoods, and exhausted our resources like there was no tomorrow. The following picture was taken at the Hungry Eye or the Domino Club while waiting for the entertainment to arrive. Wall to wall party!

We had no children, allowing the Navy experience to be unencumbered with dependents and the tribulations of child rearing. We hoped to enter into that lifestyle in the near future, leaving world travels behind. By the tender ages of 24 and 25, we had traveled the world, and had experienced first-hand exotic cultures that most persons at the time could never imagine in a lifetime.

Finally, C. S. Thomas returned to Washington, signed the needed papers, and transmitted them to Treasure Island. As my final, official act as an officer and gentleman as a Lieutenant JG, SC, U.S. Navy, I prepared and signed my own papers releasing me from active duty in the Regular Navy. If I had it to do again, I would probably repeat it exactly as it happened.

My small role in the Navy provided an awesome personal and professional experience. It included responsibilities with and for hundreds of well qualified and patriotic American sailors. The lifestyle in the 50s Navy was like no other before or since, and the American public's support of the military was unquestioned.

During seven years in the Navy, I had experienced all that had been promised and more. I served on four commissioned vessels, the USS Wisconsin, USS Missouri, USS Gardiner's Bay, and the USS Hamilton County. The drive back to Western Kansas was the beginning of a totally new, and unexplored future.

We returned to the placid lifestyle on the farm in the middle of the Western Kansas prairie, content to relax a spell following a whirlwind, seven-year tour of the world's diverse peoples, seas, and cultures. We were still just kids!!

God Bless America in the 1950s.

Made in the USA
Columbia, SC
13 January 2020